AMERICAN
WAR LIBRARY
★ ★ ★ ★

★ The Persian Gulf War ★

WEAPONS OF WAR

Titles in The American War Library series include:

World War II
Hitler and the Nazis
Kamikazes
Leaders and Generals
Life as a POW
Life of an American Soldier in
 Europe
Strategic Battles in Europe
Strategic Battles in the Pacific
The War at Home
Weapons of War

The Civil War
Leaders of the North and South
Life Among the Soldiers and
 Cavalry
Lincoln and the Abolition of
 Slavery

Strategic Battles
Weapons of War

The Persian Gulf War
Leaders and Generals
Life of an American Soldier
The War Against Iraq
Weapons of War

The Vietnam War
A History of U.S. Involvement
The Home Front: Americans
 Protest the War
Leaders and Generals
Life of an American Soldier
Life as a POW
Weapons of War

AMERICAN WAR LIBRARY
★ ★ ★ ★

★ The Persian Gulf War ★

WEAPONS OF WAR

by Jay Speakman

Lucent Books, P.O. Box 289011, San Diego, CA 92198-9011

Library of Congress Cataloging-in-Publication Data

Speakman, Jay.
    Weapons of war / by Jay Speakman
        p.   cm.—(American war library: Persian Gulf)
    Includes bibliographical references and index.
    Summary: Describes the weapons used in the Persian Gulf War
    including aircraft and ground weapons, and discusses weapons
    support, training, information, and the influence of sea power on
    Desert Storm.
        ISBN 1-56006-649-0 (hardcover)
        1. Persian Gulf War, 1991—Equipment and supplies—
    Juvenile literature. 2. Weapons systems—History—20th century—
    Juvenile literature. [1. Persian Gulf War, 1991—Equipment and
    supplies. 2. Weapons systems. 3. Military weapons.] I. Title.
    II. Series.
        DS79.723 S64   2001
        956.7044'24—dc21

00-008656

Cover photo: An A-10 Warthog aircraft flies over a target area during Operation Desert Storm.

Copyright 2001 by Lucent Books, Inc.
P.O. Box 289011, San Diego, California 92198-9011

Printed in the U.S.A.

★ Contents ★

A Nation Forged by War

The United States, like many nations, was forged and defined by war. Despite Benjamin Franklin's opinion that "There never was a good war or a bad peace," the United States owes its very existence to the War of Independence, one to which Franklin wholeheartedly subscribed. The country forged by war in 1776 was tempered and made stronger by the Civil War in the 1860s.

The Texas Revolution, the Mexican-American War, and the Spanish-American War expanded the country's borders and gave it overseas possessions. These wars made the United States a world power, but this status came with a price, as the nation became a key but reluctant player in both World War I and World War II.

Each successive war further defined the country's role on the world stage. Following World War II, U.S. foreign policy redefined itself to focus on the role of defender, not only of the freedom of its own citizens, but also of the freedom of people everywhere. During the cold war that followed World War II until the collapse of the Soviet Union, defending the world meant fighting communism. This goal, manifested in the Korean and Vietnam conflicts, proved elusive, and soured the American public on its achievability. As the United States emerged as the world's sole superpower, American foreign policy has been guided less by national interest and more on protecting international human rights. But as involvement in Somalia and Kosovo prove, this goal has been equally elusive.

As a result, the country's view of itself changed. Bolstered by victories in World Wars I and II, Americans first relished the role of protector. But, as war followed war in a seemingly endless procession, Americans began to doubt their leaders, their motives, and themselves. The Vietnam War especially caused people to question the validity of sending its young people to die in places where they were not particularly wanted and for people who did not seem especially grateful.

While the most obvious changes brought about by America's wars have been geopolitical in nature, many other aspects of society have been touched. War often does not bring about change directly, but acts instead like the catalyst in a chemical reaction, accelerating changes already in progress.

Some of these changes have been societal. The role of women in the United States had been slowly changing, but World War II put thousands into the workforce and into uniform. They might have gone back to being housewives after the war, but equality, once experienced, would not be forgotten.

Likewise, wars have accelerated technological change. The necessity for faster airplanes and a more destructive bomb led to the development of jet planes and nuclear energy. Artificial fibers developed for parachutes in the 1940s were used in the clothing of the 1950s.

Lucent Books' American War Library covers key wars in the development of the nation. Each war is covered in several volumes, to allow for more detail, context, and to provide volumes on often neglected subjects, such as the kamikazes of World War II, or weapons used in the Civil War. As with all Lucent Books, notes, annotated bibliographies, and appendixes such as glossaries give students a launching point for further research. In addition, sidebars and archival photographs enhance the text. Together, each volume in The American War Library will aid students in understanding how America's wars have shaped and changed its politics, economics, and society.

Desert Storm: The Inauguration of High-Tech War

O n August 2, 1990, Iraq invaded and occupied neighboring Kuwait, creating deep fears in the Persian Gulf region and sending shock waves out to the wider world dependent on Persian Gulf oil. Five months later, the United States led a coalition of nations in a military campaign to expel Iraq from Kuwait. Called Operation Desert Storm, the war between the U.S.-led coalition and Iraq demonstrated the awesome effects of high technology applied to warfare. The United States and its partners used an assortment of high-tech weapons to blind, paralyze, and pound Iraqi forces. The U.S.-led coalition also used airpower with devastating effect to strike military and economic targets inside Iraq itself. After six weeks of bombing and a mere four-day operation by ground forces, the United States and its allies sent Iraqi forces fleeing from Kuwait in confusion and panic. As a former U.S. diplomat later wrote, it was "one of the most complete battle-field victories in military history." [1]

Coalition Aims

"War is nothing but the continuation policy by other means," [2] wrote Carl von Clausewitz, a famous Prussian military historian. He meant that war is usually undertaken for a purpose, to accomplish certain aims. In this case, American president George Bush used force to frustrate Iraq's dangerous designs for the Persian Gulf region.

Iraq's immediate aim was straightforward: to conquer a neighbor, one rich in oil. Kuwait's oil reserves were as large as Iraq's, and by conquering Kuwait the Iraqi government in Baghdad would control nearly 20 percent of the world's oil supply. At the same time, Iraq also hoped to intimidate the rich but weak states on the Arabian Peninsula by its use of force against Kuwait. By scaring other oil producers, it might succeed in getting them to reduce oil production, keeping prices high. (Because the Iraqi economy had suffered greatly during the 1980–1988 war with Iran, Iraq was desperate for increased revenues.)

Taking possession of Kuwait's oil refineries such as this one would enable Iraq to control 20 percent of the world's oil supply.

If its conquest of Kuwait were allowed to stand unopposed, Iraq would later have the option of invading other countries, perhaps even Saudi Arabia, the biggest prize in the Persian Gulf.

For the United States, the most immediate policy objective was to protect its close friend Saudi Arabia from Iraqi aggression. Immediately after deploying protection forces to Saudi Arabia, the United States went to work building the coalition, which would first apply political and economic pressure and then military pressure on Iraq to drive its occupation force from Kuwait. When Iraq showed no signs of yielding after

five months of economic sanctions imposed by the UN Security Council, the U.S.-led coalition decided to use force to restore Kuwait's independence and to defend regional security and stability.

Weapons and Strategies

Though much weaker than the United States, Iraq did have some advantages. Military power diminishes with distance, and the United States was far away from Kuwait while Iraq was next door. For a medium-size country, Iraq boasted many advanced weapons. Iraq's first line of defense, its air-defense system, was large and sophisticated. In Kuwait, the Iraqis laid thousands of mines, strongly fortified their positions, and deployed a variety of weapons. Iraq possessed Soviet Scud missiles and its own modified version of Scuds, both capable of striking targets at a distance of two hundred to four hundred miles. It could use these to attack U.S. forces in Saudi Arabia. It could also use them to attack Israel in hopes of drawing Israel into the war, which might create fissures within the U.S.-led coalition. There were also threats that Iraq would carry out terrorist attacks, take hostages, or employ chemical weapons either against Israel or against American forces in Saudi Arabia.

Iraq's defensive and offensive weapons confronted the United States and its allies with a formidable challenge. When war actually came, it proved to be a rout. Beforehand, however, it was far from clear that victory would be so easy. Surveying Iraqi air and ground defenses (plus Iraq's offensive threats), coalition planners had to reckon with the possibility that the Iraqis might be able to down hundreds of coalition aircraft and impose casualties numbering in the tens of thousands.

Several factors account for Iraq's inability to turn its defensive advantages into a tough fight. First, in a stunning display of high-tech warfare, the U.S.-led coalition was able to use modern, sophisticated weapons to devastating effect. Second, overwhelming material advantages allowed the United States to call on forces and military support that Iraq could not possibly match. And third, the superior training and support of the U.S.-led forces enabled the coalition to prevail in battle even in instances when Iraqi weapons were essentially comparable to coalition ones.

The Defeat of Iraq

The coalition's technological and material advantages proved overwhelming in combat. The coalition initiated hostilities against Iraqi forces on January 17, 1991. After crippling Iraq's air defenses, it waged

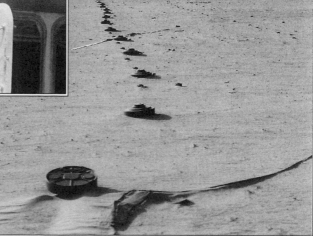

Iraq's defensive efforts, including antiaircraft guns (above) and land mines (right) proved futile against coalition attacks.

an intensive air campaign against Iraqi command centers, and communications links, troops, military equipment, power and transportation links, war supplies (such as fuel for Iraqi tanks and other military vehicles), Scud missiles, and weapons-of-mass-destruction facilities. After six weeks of ferocious attacks from the air, Iraqi forces were gravely weakened by the bombing and "blinded" by the destruction of their intelligence and communications systems.

The coalition then initiated warfare on the ground. Moving straight up from Kuwait and in a two-prong offensive to the west, directly from Saudi Arabia into Iraq itself, coalition ground forces used superior tanks and artillery, supported by lethal groups of fighter aircraft, to overrun and outflank Iraqi forces. A great flanking maneuver far to the west (dubbed the "Hail Mary" maneuver) swept across hundreds of miles of desert, taking Basra in southeastern Iraq and cutting off the remaining Iraqi forces in Kuwait in the process.

After six weeks of bombing and a four-day ground assault, it was all over. Although some criticized President Bush for not sending coalition forces to Baghdad to overthrow the government of Iraqi president Saddam Hussein, Desert Storm was a complete success in driving Iraqi forces from Kuwait. A mere thirty-seven coalition planes were lost to combat (and fifteen more to operational mishaps), and only 146 Americans were killed in combat. And civilian casualties in Iraq were very low.

This is the story of how the well-trained forces of the United States and its partners used sophisticated weapons to achieve such an overwhelming success.

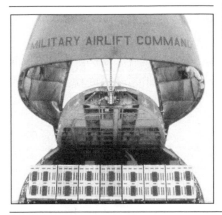

Chapter 1

Projecting Power and Preparing for War

Iraq's invasion of Kuwait was swift and brutal. Spearheaded by armored and mechanized divisions, Iraq's invading army of 140,000 quickly captured the smaller country's capital, Kuwait City. Kuwait's leader, the emir, barely escaped capture before he fled to Saudi Arabia to establish a government in exile. Kuwait's small army and air force bravely resisted the larger Iraqi forces until they ran out of fuel and ammunition several days later.

American Responses and Goals

Iraq's invasion posed a serious challenge to the United States. The invasion was a flagrant violation of international law. Iraq's brutal occupation of Kuwait was a terrible ordeal for the Kuwaiti people. By bringing Kuwait's oil wealth under Iraqi control, the invasion threatened to increase revenues that Iraq could use to enlarge its already substantial military power, including ambitious programs to develop weapons of mass destruction (WMD)—nuclear, chemical, and biological weapons. The invasion also raised the prospect of further Iraqi aggression in the Persian Gulf region. Saudi Arabia was the most obvious and tempting target because it was militarily weak and possessed the world's largest proven reserves of oil. Israel was also a likely target. Iraq was not capable of a direct attack on Israel, but it could strike Israeli population centers with its long-range Scud missiles, which might conceivably be armed with warheads carrying chemical weapons.

For all of these reasons, President Bush declared that Iraq's aggression "will not stand."[3] The American president hoped the crisis would be settled peacefully. And that, under the pressure of diplomatic isolation and UN-mandated economic sanctions, Iraq might just leave Kuwait, avoiding bloodshed. If the United States had to use force, however, President Bush intended to pursue additional goals. In addition to pushing Iraq out of Kuwait, the

The Iraqi occupation of Kuwait that began on August 2, 1990, proved brutal. Pictured are Iraqi soldiers and one of their tanks in front of a damaged mosque in Kuwait City.

United States and its coalition partners would attempt to destroy Iraq's WMD programs and to batter Iraqi armed forces hard enough to reduce Iraq's future threat to peace and stability in the Persian Gulf. Under the best of circumstances, the war would lead to Iraqi president Saddam Hussein's overthrow or death.

It would take time, however, to push Iraq out of Kuwait. For Bush the most immediate problem was the Iraqi threat to his ally Saudi Arabia. It seemed very possible that Iraqi forces in Kuwait might keep moving south, invading Saudi Arabia itself. Thus, rapid American action was impera-tive. Within days, Operation Desert Shield, a large-scale military deployment to protect Saudi Arabia, was underway.

U.S. Ties to the Persian Gulf

For decades, the United States had recognized the vital importance of the Persian Gulf region. Because of the region's great oil wealth, developments there could seriously damage the economic welfare and national security of many nations, including the United States.

The United States had long-standing ties to the Gulf, and in 1980 it had formally committed itself to the defense of the region under the so-called Carter Doctrine. President Jimmy Carter created the Rapid Deployment Force (RDF) to conduct military operations in the area, and in 1983, under President Ronald Reagan, an expanded RDF became a full-fledged U.S. military command called Central Command (CENTCOM). Naval and airborne forces were dedicated to missions in the Persian Gulf. Numerous training missions were carried out over the years, both in the western deserts of the United States and in the Middle East, to prepare CENTCOM for a range of possible threats.

Over the years CENTCOM became an impressive fighting force. One major shortcoming confronting it, however, was the absence of military infrastructure in the Persian Gulf. Because of political sensitivities, no Gulf nation would allow U.S. bases or a large U.S. military presence in the region. The United States could redeploy some forces from Europe to the Gulf, and it did have access to the small island of Diego Garcia in the Indian Ocean, where it kept ships and stockpiles of supplies. Diego Garcia is not exactly close to the Gulf, though. In fact, it is twenty-five hundred miles away. But that still makes it six thousand miles closer to the Persian Gulf than the United States. Most forces would have to come from the United States, which is

nine thousand miles from the Gulf by sea, six thousand miles by air.

To protect Saudi Arabia, the United States would have to create a large-scale military presence in that country very quickly. Over a longer period, an even larger military buildup would be necessary to drive Iraqi forces from Kuwait. Meeting these demands at such great distances posed a serious challenge to the Bush administration.

Military Support: Getting Forces in Place

Washington's aim was to put a brigade of fifteen thousand marines in Saudi Arabia by late August 1990. By early fall, U.S. forces there totaled two hundred thousand. By the end of the year that number was five hundred thousand. But getting troops there was only a small part of the challenge. Without weapons, fuel, food, medicine, ammunition, and other equipment, soldiers are useless.

The art of supplying war is called logistics. Keeping armies supplied is always difficult, and keeping them well supplied at great distances is extremely difficult. The United States is the only country in the world capable of projecting great power at large distances.

A half million American troops needed vast quantities of weapons and supplies. The needs were especially great because the United States, more than any other country, tries to ensure that its soldiers have ample supplies of everything—from the little things that can make a soldier's life more pleasant (exercise equipment, American brands of food, etc.) to the big things that win battles and save lives, such as vast quantities of weapons and ammunition and state-of-the-art medical supplies.

Most combat aircraft (except helicopters) could be piloted rather than transported to the Gulf. Even so, the transport needs for large weapons systems were immense. For instance, only America's mammoth C-5 Galaxy cargo plane could carry the M1A1 Abrams tank, and even the C-5 could only carry one tank (at most two) per flight. The transport needs of ammunition alone amounted to 350,000 tons. Vast quantities of fuel were needed to keep ships, tanks, and planes in operation, and fuel is quite heavy.

Both planes and ships were used to transport troops and equipment to the Kuwaiti theater of operations (KTO).

Airlift

Especially in the early stages of deployment, soldiers and some weapons and supplies must be moved rapidly into the theater of conflict. This was certainly the case in the Persian Gulf in the initial weeks after Iraq's invasion of Kuwait. Consequently, airlift was an important part of the logistical equation.

The United States provided the lion's share of both the coalition's military equipment and the lift needed to get that equipment to the Persian Gulf. The air force had two types of aircraft to carry tanks and other heavy equipment. One was the C-141 Starlifter, which needed two midair refuelings to fly nonstop to the Gulf carrying about forty tons of equipment. At the height of the buildup, two hundred Starlifters were in operation, flying an average of about twelve hours per day. The other cargo plane was the immense C-5 Galaxy, the third largest plane in the world. Each of the ninety-six C-5s could carry three times the cargo of the C-141.

The air force worked with the commercial airlines to get troops into the Gulf. Altogether, military and civilian aircraft flew fifteen thousand flights, bringing about five hundred thousand troops and six hundred thousand tons of equipment into the theater of combat.

Sealift

Although transporting troops and supplies by air is fast, it is much more expensive than transporting them by sea, which is known as sealift. Therefore, sealift is the key to power projection. Fully 95 percent of the equipment and supplies sent to the Persian Gulf for Operations Desert Shield and Desert Storm were transported by sea.

As part of its decade-plus preparations for possible conflicts in the Persian Gulf region, the United States had ten large ships, called maritime prepositioning ships (MPSs), permanently stationed at Diego Garcia. In a week's sailing time, those ten ships were able to deliver hundreds of trucks, tanks, and artillery to Saudi Arabia. The MPS fleet also carried thirty days'

To transport heavy equipment and supplies to the Persian Gulf, the U.S. Air Force utilized the C-141 Starlifter (left) and the C-5 Galaxy (right).

worth of food, medical supplies, and ammunition to sustain the first brigade of marines who were sent to Saudi Arabia from the United States.

The United States also employed eight large high-speed cargo ships. These ships were capable of carrying tanks and other heavy equipment. Additionally, the United States had two dozen ships loaded with equipment for ground forces. The U.S. military had contracts with the owners of two hundred private merchant ships, which shipped 7 million tons of supplies to the Persian Gulf.

In less than six months' time, the United States and other coalition members were able to construct an immense military machine, right next door to Iraqi-occupied Kuwait. Almost from scratch, an army of more than a half million soldiers was put in place. Huge army and air bases were created and heavily stocked with weapons, ammunition, and air bases were created and heavily stocked with weapons, am-

munition, and other supplies. Sealift was the key to this immense buildup. By facilitating this Herculean movement of military forces and supplies, sealift made the coalition's eventual victory possible.

Getting forces to the region was the biggest challenge, but not the only one. Even after the troops, weapons, and supplies reached the Persian Gulf, there were

still huge transport needs. From ports and airports, the vast coalition military machine had to move to bases in Saudi Arabia and to a series of defensive points along the border between Saudi Arabia and Kuwait.

The U.S. Navy sent eight large cargo ships to carry heavy equipment such as this M1A1 Abrams tank to the Persian Gulf.

Theater Mobility

Moving forces from ports and airports to their actual destination is called "theater" or "tactical" lift. To perform this mission, the coalition needed thousands of transport planes, helicopters, and trucks.

The C-130 Hercules was the workhorse of the short-range transport planes. Old but rugged and highly reliable, the four-engine C-130 can carry a forty-five-thousand-pound cargo more than two thousand miles. The four-propeller plane can use short, bumpy airstrips. The C-130 is also one of the world's most versatile airplanes, with converted versions used to fight forest fires, gather intelligence, and fight as gunships. Two hundred C-130s were used in the Gulf. Before and during the war, the airspace around coalition military installations was constantly buzzing with the droning turboprop engines of the Hercules.

Hundreds of helicopters carried smaller loads than the Hercules did, but they were more versatile because of their ability to take off and land almost anywhere. The U.S. Army relied mainly on some 300 older Huey light-transport helicopters, which could carry about a dozen soldiers or four thousand pounds of supplies; almost 400 of the more modern Blackhawk medium-lift (and combat-support) helicopters, which transported fourteen troops or nine thousand pounds of equipment; and 150 Chinook heavy-transport helicopters, which could move fifty-five troops or twenty-seven thousand pounds of equipment. The marines used similar helicopters, approximately 200 medium-lift Sea Knights and heavy-lift Sea Stallions.

The coalition also employed thousands of trucks to move troops and equipment around the KTO. Taken as a whole, the theater lift gave the coalition great flexibility in military deployments and ensured that coalition forces were amply supplied with wartime needs. When the combat phase began, the coalition's theater lift enabled its forces to combine intense firepower and rapid mobility, outflanking and overrunning Iraqi defensive positions.

Truck Shortages and Improvising Solutions

Once equipment reached the Gulf, it had to be moved to numerous positions in Saudi Arabia and elsewhere. The need for transport trucks and drivers was immense. At the beginning of the buildup, when it appeared that Iraq might invade Saudi Arabia as well as Kuwait, the coalition simply was not able to meet that huge need. So, commanders improvised. They rented trucks where they could find them, hastily spray-painting "Rented to the U.S. Army, Op. Desert Shield" on their sides. At the same time, U.S. Army officers recruited truck drivers from around the region. Soon, they had a legion of Pakistani, Indian, Korean, and Filipino drivers who were suited up with camouflage caps and T-shirts with a Desert Shield logo. Working under U.S. Army officers, these drivers performed very well, though some of their habits seemed a bit strange to the American soldiers. Since many of the contract drivers were Muslims, they had to stop their trucks five times a day while they prayed. The Americans had no difficulty getting used to these stops. They were, however, uncomfortable when the trucks stopped so that the non-American drivers could make their afternoon tea. An American colonel explains why in the book *Triumph Without Victory: The Unreported History of the Persian Gulf War*, compiled by the staff of *U.S. News & World Report.*

They would always build their fire in the shade, and the only shade was under their truck trailer. So you had these guys building little fires with their propane heaters under a truck loaded with artillery ammunition or explosives. And this guy is under the truck cooking his tea, and the GI is out there in the sand a ways away because he knows that truck is going to go boom. Never lost one, though. They were a great team.

Overall, U.S. lift capabilities negated one of Iraq's few advantages: proximity to the combat area. Although the United States was many thousands of miles away, American lift capabilities allowed the United States to create a military machine much more powerful than Iraq's.

Because of America's lift capabilities, the Desert Shield buildup to protect Saudi Arabia proceeded quickly. The force of a half million in Saudi Arabia by the end of the year was much larger than what was needed to defend the country. The Iraqis understood that this large, well-supplied army was poised to wage offensive operations against their forces in Kuwait. Offensive action seemed all the more likely because the United States had succeeded in building a broad coalition of nations against Iraq and in getting the UN Security Council to pass a series of resolutions against Iraq. The most important UN resolution authorized all nations to use all necessary means—a diplomatic phrase meaning the use of force—to get Iraq out of Kuwait after a deadline of January 15.

Iraq's Weapons of Deterrence

The challenge to Iraq was straightforward. Iraq had to consolidate its position in Kuwait to make American intervention unbearably costly. Saddam Hussein clearly did not wish for a war with the United States. He knew that Iraq could not defeat the United States, but he hoped that the prospect of a tough fight would deter U.S.

officials from initiating war over Kuwait. Hussein believed that the United States did not have the stomach for a long, bloody war and that, with a strong defensive position in Kuwait, Iraq could threaten the U.S.-led coalition with just such a prolonged and costly conflict. Hussein could also use several forms of unconventional warfare to increase military casualties and make Western civilians targets of war. As he built those defenses, the Iraqi dictator bragged that the United States would face the "mother of all battles" and threatened that "not a few drops of blood, but rivers of blood would be shed."[4]

Air Defenses and Fortifications

Iraq anticipated that the United States would start with a campaign of bombing. Thus, its first task was to fortify its air defenses in both Kuwait and Iraq. With a very dense and overlapping system of early-warning radars, antiaircraft missiles, antiaircraft artillery (called AAA or Triple-A), other antiaircraft guns and flak, and interceptor jet fighters, Hussein could hope to make the skies very hot for American warplanes. With a stout air defense, the Iraqis could hope to deter or absorb U.S. air strikes, minimizing damage to its forces and to its command and control system—the eyes, ears, and brains of any military operation. Baghdad could also hope to shoot down U.S. planes, creating casualties and prisoners of war and thereby putting pressure on the Bush administration to abandon military operations.

In Kuwait, the Iraqis laid thousands of mines and strongly fortified their positions. They dug trenches, built tank traps, created concrete bunkers and large sand berms, and actually buried tanks in the ground, gun barrels out, so they would be harder to destroy. Behind their defensive lines, the Iraqis deployed thousands of tanks, armored personnel carriers, and artillery pieces. Further back, Iraq's best troops, the elite Republican Guard, waited for the opportunity to launch a punishing counterattack if coalition forces stalled upon encountering the first lines of Iraqi defenses.

Terror, Hostages, and Human Shields

While defensive efforts represented the main element in Iraqi strategy, Baghdad could supplement those efforts with several unconventional forms of warfare. One was terrorism. Groups acting on behalf of Iraq could infiltrate the United States or other coalition countries and blow up public buildings, assassinate leaders, hijack planes, or set off explosions in crowded places. As its name implies, terrorism is intended to instill terror in the hearts of its intended victims, putting whole societies on edge. The "weapon" of terrorism is not very sophisticated or costly, and it certainly cannot produce military victories, but it is a potent weapon, nonetheless.

It is, however, a double-edged sword. Acts of terrorism in the weeks before Desert Storm would have angered and alienated many of those who were even marginally sympathetic to Iraq. Worse yet, terrorist incidents might well have provoked the very coalition attack that the Iraqis hoped to deter. On the other hand, once hostilities commenced, Iraqi leaders would be too preoccupied with the war to direct terrorist activities abroad and their physical ability to do so would be degraded by coalition attacks on their communication systems. Iraqi leaders also had to worry that terrorist incidents might result in increased ferocity of coalition attacks and perhaps more concerted efforts to overthrow, capture, or kill Iraqi leaders. To Iraq's further disadvantage, in the months leading up to Desert Storm, Western intelligence agencies were able to devote substantial resources to uncovering and thwarting Iraqi-sponsored terrorist operations.

In Kuwait, the Iraqis detained hundreds of European civilians, implying that they would be held hostage and perhaps harmed in the event of a U.S. attack. Fortunately for the West, this potentially potent weapon was never used. Weeks before the coalition's air campaign began, the Iraqi government allowed Western civilians to leave Iraq in the hope that such a gesture of so-called good will would prevent a coalition attack.

Kuwaiti citizens were not so lucky. The Iraqis used thousands of Kuwaiti men as human shields in front of their military equipment, confronting coalition planners with the prospect of killing the very people they were attempting to save.

Hostages and Human Shields

Thousands of Western civilians, mostly Europeans, lived in Iraq. Many were businesspeople who had their families with them. The Iraqi government believed their presence could be used as a weapon against Western governments contemplating military action against Iraq. By simply declaring that foreigners could not leave the country, Iraq turned those foreign civilians into hostages. The Iraqi government neither called Western civilians "hostages" nor made explicit threats against them; that was unnecessary. All it had to do was make vague statements that could only be construed as threats.

The holding of hostages served three purposes for Iraq. First, it could use them to deter attacks on specific sites that were likely to be targeted by the United States and its allies. Male hostages were taken to military sites to act as human shields, both in Iraq and occupied Kuwait. Second, Baghdad hoped that the detention of hundreds of foreigners might deter the United States and others from using force altogether. Western governments would have to contend with the grim fact that hostages could be harmed, tortured, or even killed. A televised meeting between Saddam Hussein and a group of Western "guests," in which Hussein patted a small British boy on the head, sent a chilling message about Iraq's control over the fate of the Westerners. And third, Iraq could use the hostages to create divisions between coalition members by releasing the citizens of some countries and not others.

The United States and other governments demanded the release of the civilians and declared that they would not be deterred from taking the necessary measures to get Iraq out of Kuwait. But they were clearly worried. Hussein had a reputation for ruthlessness, and no government wanted to take actions that would result in harm coming to hostages. For many weeks, a parade of current and former world leaders and other prominent people journeyed to Baghdad seeking the release of the hostages. In the face of U.S. efforts to isolate Iraq diplomatically, this tribute to Hussein's power had to be pleasing to the Iraqi dictator.

Ultimately, Iraq decided the hostage game was not worth the trouble. Because of its invasion of Kuwait, Iraq had few friends or supporters. By holding hostages, Iraq further angered other governments, making it easier for the United States to gain approval for anti-Iraq resolutions at the United Nations. Even countries sympathetic to Iraq urged Hussein to release the hostages. Many in the Arab world considered it especially cowardly to use women and children as hostages.

The Iraqi dictator backtracked. In October the Iraqi government announced that women and children would be free to leave Iraq. This still left some six hundred men as hostages and human shields. Soon, however, Hussein retreated further on the issue. Under pressure and hoping that the release of all hostages would discourage some countries from endorsing military action, Iraq announced in early December that all Westerners were free to leave the country. After this, Iraq no longer had a hostage "weapon" to use against the coalition.

Chemical Weapons and Scud Missiles

Small powers can seldom fight great powers on even terms. Any country facing a larger, better-armed foe has to devise a strategy that takes this into account. One way for Iraq to confront the United States with the risk of unacceptably high casualties was with the threat of deadly chemical warfare. For Iraq, nuclear or biological (germ) threats would have been more effective because of their potential to kill thousands of U.S. soldiers. But Iraq was still a year away from developing a nuclear weapon, and although the Iraqis did have a large germ-warfare program, they had not overcome the technological challenge of placing germs in a warhead that would disperse the still-living organisms among enemy soldiers.

Iraq did, however, possess chemical weapons. And the United States had to assume that Iraq was capable of firing either long-range Scud missiles or short-range FROG (free rocket over ground) missiles fitted with chemical warheads. Missiles gave Iraq the potential to strike American forces either on the battlefield or on military bases in Saudi Arabia. The same missiles, armed with either chemical weapons or high explosives, could be used against Saudi Arabia—as punishment for cooperating with the United States—or against Israel. Having already used chemical weapons against Iranians and against its own population (killing five thousand in one deadly attack), the Iraqi government obviously had ex-

perience with them. In fact, after Desert Storm was over, U.S. military analysts concluded that Iraq had indeed had the ability to place chemical warheads on Scud missiles.

Iraq's Position

The Iraqis had reasons to be hopeful. Despite the enormous wealth and technological superiority of the United States, Iraq seemed prepared to wage a stubborn fight to keep Kuwait. Its large army was well

Although Iraq was a year away from developing nucler weapons, it did have chemical weapons that could have been deployed on Scud missiles.

equipped with heavy weapons. Its air defenses seemed poised to fill the sky with walls of fire. Hundreds of attacking fighters and bombers might be destroyed. With thousands of artillery pieces and tanks and other armored vehicles, Iraq was prepared to greet coalition forces with immense firepower. Its Scud missiles could deliver high explosives or even chemical weapons behind enemy lines or into Israel. Iraq could threaten to harm hostages or unleash terrorists against the West. And, it could threaten Kuwaitis with widespread death and destruction and with an economic and ecological catastrophe by setting hundreds of Kuwaiti oil wells ablaze.

The actual conflict that started on January 17, 1991 went very well for the United States and its coalition allies. But this was by no means clear beforehand. In fact, Iraq's strategy of deterrence almost worked. James Baker, who was the U.S. secretary of state (the president's main foreign policy adviser) at the time, later acknowledged that the decision to intervene was very difficult. According to Baker, the United States "confronted very sobering casualty figures, estimated by the Pentagon to be in the thousands; the specter of possible chemical and biological attacks; and a war expected to last for months, not days."[5] In fact, early figures by the U.S. Department of Defense, or Pentagon, estimated that the United States might suffer casualties of forty thousand dead and wounded. The Pentagon also estimated that Iraq might be able to shoot down 150 coalition warplanes on the first night of the attack and hundreds more during the conflict.

Despite deep concerns about potential casualties, President Bush decided that Iraq had to be forced out of Kuwait. The key to success would be a massive bombing campaign. Before undertaking this campaign, however, the coalition would have to seize control of the skies over Kuwait and Iraq.

Chapter 2

The Weapons
of Air
Domination

Operation Desert Storm began with air strikes in the early morning hours of January 17, two days after the UN deadline for Iraq's withdrawal from Kuwait had passed without Iraqi compliance. Before the full-scale bombing campaign could begin, the coalition would have to destroy Iraqi air defenses and neutralize its air force. Since Iraq's air-defense weapons were extensive and quite sophisticated, this was a very demanding mission.

Iraq's Air Defenses

Iraq seemed well poised to mount a strong defense. At the start of the 1990s, Iraq had one of the world's largest and most sophisticated air-defense systems, much of it acquired from its Soviet friends. Iraq had what is called an integrated air-defense system (IADS). As the term *integrated* suggests, the components of the system were all designed to work together.

Iraq's IADS was thick with radar systems. Some radar would detect high-flying enemy aircraft, and some would locate low-flying attackers. Different types of radar could cover narrow and wide areas and greater and lesser distances outward. Taken together, the radar systems would provide overlapping and duplicating coverage so that if one system were destroyed, another would still cover the same area. Some radar systems were mobile, which made them hard to find and destroy. Unfortunately for the Iraqis, some systems could not be moved. For instance, their main early-warning radar, called "Tall King," was not mobile.

Radar detection of incoming aircraft was, of course, just the first step. The second was to attack and destroy invading planes. Iraq possessed a large array of antiaircraft weapons. The most common defensive weapon was the antiaircraft gun. At the start of the war, Iraq was believed to have seven thousand of them. The most numerous were little more than machine guns, sometimes mounted atop buildings

The first goal of the coalition was to disable the radar systems of Iraq's integrated air-defense system (IADS).

system was under the central control of Iraq's high-level military command. Integration and central control were important to prevent Iraqi fighters from being mistaken and attacked as enemy aircraft.

The Iraqis also hoped to defend themselves against coalition air strikes with fighters (also called interceptors) and fighter-bombers. By the standards of a fairly small country, Iraq had a large, modernized air force. It had more than 500 interceptors and fighter-bombers. Its best fighters included 116 French Mirage F-1s and 48 Soviet MiG-29s. The Mirage was a dependable and effective fighter even though it had been developed twenty years earlier. The newer MiG-29 was a first-rate combat aircraft. It carried a thirty millimeter cannon and up to six missiles for air-to-air combat. It could fly at Mach 2.3, more than twice the speed of sound. And, it was very maneuverable. On a good day, with a skilled pilot, the MiG-29 was capable of defeating any coalition aircraft.

Iraq was expecting the beginning of military operations anytime after January 15, and it was thus alert and ready for the onset of the air war. Because of this, and because of Iraq's extensive, modernized air-defense system, there was a great deal of nervous tension both in the Persian Gulf and in Washington, D.C., on the eve of the war.

in Baghdad. The larger and more effective guns were antiaircraft artillery. Iraq's most deadly defense against attacking coalition aircraft was the surface-to-air missile (SAMs), mostly of Soviet design. Moving at supersonic speeds and employing a variety of sophisticated targeting devices, Iraq's ten thousand SAMs posed a serious threat to all kinds of coalition aircraft.

Like the radar systems, the air-defense weapons were part of an integrated system, offering protection from aircraft attacking at any altitude. Low-flying enemy aircraft could be attacked by antiaircraft guns or short-range, low-altitude SAMs. Against high-altitude attackers, the Iraqis could use fighters or long-range missiles. Much of the

Iraqi Antiaircraft Weapons

Iraq fielded more than ten thousand antiaircraft artillery pieces. About two hundred towed guns fired large shells—85, 100, and 130 millimeters in diameter. Most were lighter. Iraq's best antiaircraft artillery were Soviet systems, called the ZSU 57-2 and ZSU 23-24. Both were mobile and both could rapidly create a dangerous wall of fire in the path of incoming aircraft. The ZSU 57-2 was a twin 57-millimeter cannon mounted on a tank frame and capable of firing about one hundred rounds per minute. The ZSU 23-24 carried four smaller cannons mounted on another kind of self-propelled armored vehicle, each gun capable of firing up to one thousand rounds per minute. These guns could hit aircraft flying twenty-four thousand feet or lower at a range of about seven miles.

More dangerous were Iraq's thousands of surface-to-air missiles (SAMs). Some could fly at more than twice the speed of sound. Low-altitude missiles could hit planes as low as thirty feet off the ground. High-altitude missiles could reach targets several miles in the air. A few of the SAMs relied on optical sights for locating their targets. Most had their own target-acquisition radars.

The missiles employed several targeting technologies. Some followed a radio beam to their targets; others used radar guidance; still others relied on sensors that would zero in on the heat from the exhaust of enemy planes. Some of the high-explosive warheads on the SAMs could be designed to detonate on impact with targets, close to targets, or by a radio signal from commanders on the ground. Most SAMs were mounted on trucks or armored vehicles, some in pairs or even fours. Three of the missiles (SA-7s, -14s, and -16s) were fired from shoulder-mounted tubes that resembled bazookas. The small shoulder-fired missiles were extremely difficult to find and destroy (except when they were being fired), and were thus a threat throughout the conflict. Coalition aircraft were well suited to evading, confusing, and destroying Iraq's SAMs. Nonetheless, the sheer number of missiles, plus the variety in their operational characteristics, made them a real threat.

Because their small size and mobility made many of Iraq's SAMs (surface-to-air missiles) difficult to find and destroy, they posed a serious threat.

Stealth Fighters and Cruise Missiles Deliver the Opening Blows

Some of the most important targets were located in Baghdad. Unfortunately, Baghdad was the second most heavily defended city in the world, after Moscow in the Soviet Union. Coalition planners had to choose the means of attack that would be least likely to fall victim to the sixty batteries of SAMs and three thousand antiaircraft guns defending Baghdad. Because of the city's dense population and the coalition's determination to keep civilian casualties as low as possible, pinpoint accuracy was also a critical requirement. Only two weapons systems met the twin demands of survivability and accuracy, the F-117A stealth Nighthawk fighter/attack plane and cruise missiles.

The F-117A

An expensive aircraft, the stealth fighter had been designed for missions like this. It is made of a composite, or mixture, of advanced materials that absorb rather than reflect radar beams, making the aircraft almost impossible to detect. Not only elusive to radar, the F-117A recycles and cools its hot exhaust fumes, making it invisible to heat-detecting sensors, including those guiding antiaircraft missiles. Engine noise is muffled so its approach cannot be heard from a distance. Flying at night, the black plane cannot be seen by defenders scanning the skies from the ground. Because of these stealthy qualities, it did not need to be accompanied by fighter escorts. Consequently, eight F-117As and two refueling tankers could do the job of seventy-five attack and support aircraft.

Though the F-117A is difficult to detect, it does produce a "signature," a blip on enemy radar screens, even though it is a tiny one. Under the right conditions, radar operators can get lucky and find the F-117A. Thus, for added insurance, coalition commanders sent several EF-111

Nearly impossible to detect, the F-117A stealth Nighthawk fighter utilized sophisticated target-finding equipment to make the air attack on Iraq swift and effective.

Raven electronic warfare planes to accompany the F-117As. The Ravens jammed Iraqi radar to make sure that none of the stealth fighters was detected. The radar jamming did alert the Iraqis to the onset of the attack, but only moments later the Nighthawks' bombs began going off. In response, the Iraqis blindly unleashed great salvos of flak and antiaircraft fire, but none of the stealth fighters was hit.

The F-117A met the other need for strikes against targets in a city of 5 million: accuracy. The Nighthawk's sophisticated target-finding equipment zeroes in on the target, which is "painted" with a laser beam. The bomb follows the laser to the target, often with pinpoint accuracy. A handful of laser-guided bombs can hit and destroy targets without causing great damage to untargeted areas. In earlier wars, in contrast, the only way targets could be reliably hit was by saturation bombing—repeated and massive strikes—which usually took a terrible toll in civilian casualties.

Cruise Missiles

Like stealth fighters, cruise missiles could penetrate Iraqi air defenses and strike targets with precision. Additionally, the use of cruise missiles put no pilots' lives at risk. As the F-117As were hitting targets in Baghdad, cruise missiles were also homing in on targets in the capital city. Most of the cruise missiles used against Iraq were Tomahawks, and these were launched from U.S. ships in the Red Sea and Persian Gulf. Seventeen vessels provided the platforms for the at-

tacks by the deadly and unstoppable Tomahawk cruise missiles. For the first time, an attack submarine, the USS *Louisville*, was

A Quick Guide to Aircraft Designations

Many U.S. warplanes are designated by one or two letters, followed by a number, and sometimes by another letter: F-117A, for example. The first letter indicates the type of aircraft: *A* is for "attack," *B* is for "bomber," *C* is for "cargo," *E* is for "electronic," *F* is for "fighter," *K* is for "tanker" (since the letter *T* refers to Soviet tanks), *R* is for "reconnaissance," and *X* is for "experimental." Some designations are a bit loose. For instance, the F-111 is really a bomber, not a fighter, and the F-117A stealth fighter is really an attack plane, not a fighter. Some planes that perform two missions get two letters, such as the navy's F/A-18 Hornet, which is a fighter-attack plane. Planes that are converted from their primary use can also get two letters. For example, C-130 cargo planes have been modified to serve a number of missions, including attack (the AC-130 gunship) and tanker (KC-130).

Planes' numbers signify little. Usually, newer planes have higher numbers. The letter that follows the number (as in F-15E) designates the model of a particular aircraft. The letters are assigned alphabetically, in sequence. An upgraded version of a particular plane gets a higher letter than the earlier versions.

Warplanes are also assigned names, typically ones that capture important physical or operational features of the plane. The powerful, high-flying B-52 is the Stratofortress. The C-130 Hercules carries great loads. The F-111 Aardvark has a snout resembling that of the African mammal. Birds of prey are favorite sources for the names of fighters: the F-15 Eagle (or, even more descriptively, Screaming Eagle), the F-16 Falcon, and the new F-22 Raptor.

also used to launch Tomahawks. Likewise, B-52 bombers fired air-launched cruise missiles.

Even though its earliest versions were developed by Nazi Germany over a half century ago, the cruise missile is one of the wonder weapons of modern warfare. About twenty feet long, with small fins and wings, and propelled by a jet engine, this missile carries a one-thousand-pound warhead of high explosives. Using several sophisticated guidance systems, the missile finds its target by "looking" at the ground with sensors and a television camera and then by matching the ground with digitized terrain maps gathered by satellite and stored in computers inside the missile. Though much slower than rockets, the five-hundred-mile-an-hour cruise missile eludes defenses by zigzagging and flying at tree-top level, underneath enemy radar.

The importance of the highly accurate, pilotless cruise missile is evident in the numbers used in the opening stages of the air war, when most of Iraq's air defenses were still in place. Of the three hundred Tomahawks used throughout the conflict, about half were devoted to critical targets in the first twenty-four hours of the air war.

Punching a Hole in Iraqi Defenses

The first waves of attacks were delivered by thirty F-117As, fifty-four Tomahawk cruise missiles launched from U.S. naval vessels, and thirty-five air-launched cruise missiles fired by huge B-52 bombers. In the first five minutes of the coalition's attack, cruise missiles and two-thousand-pound laser-guided bombs from two stealth attack planes slammed into twenty targets in Baghdad. Communication and command centers, the Ministry of Defense, Iraqi air force headquarters, and air defenses were all hit. Tomahawk cruise missiles armed with specially designed long filaments attacked the area's power grid. The filaments became wrapped up in power lines, creating short circuits in electrical transformers and causing massive power outages. Within the first twenty-four hours, almost fifty major command and control targets in the Baghdad area had been hit. At this point, the Iraqis must have realized that they were facing a uniquely powerful foe.

However, although stealth fighters and cruise missiles could fly right through Iraq's defenses, most coalition aircraft could not. Therefore, a gap had to be created in Iraq's radar system. Helicopters were assigned to carry out this first anti-radar mission.

Flying in the dark of night, three air force special operations helicopters, called Pave Lows, led nine army Apache attack helicopters on a flight just above the desert floor into southern Iraq. Their targets were two early-warning radar sites. By destroying both, they would create a blind spot in Iraq's radar coverage. A large wave of coalition attack aircraft could then fly through the narrow, blind corridor in Iraq's defenses. The Pave Low helicopters used radar and special night-vision devices to hug the ground, too low to be detected by

The battleship USS Missouri *fires a cruise missile. This weapon carries a one-thousand-pound warhead of high explosives and travels at five hundred miles an hour.*

Iraqi radar. Using precise navigational signals from global positioning system satellites, they could find their way directly to the Iraqi targets. Computerized mapping systems; forward-looking infrared radar systems, which "see" upcoming objects by their heat; and night-vision goggles enabled the attackers to find their targets.

The attack required split-second timing. It went flawlessly. Within seconds of each other, the two radar sites were destroyed. The Apaches destroyed the main buildings with Hellfire missiles. Then they fired rockets containing thousands of darts, called flechettes, to disable trucks, wiring systems, and other components of the radar sites. The Apaches finished the job with their thirty millimeter cannon. Mission accomplished, the Pave Lows and Apaches returned to Saudi Arabia. As the helicopters left Iraqi airspace, they passed underneath an armada of coalition attack planes already heading for the newly created hole in Iraq's radar coverage.

Decoys and Drones

This swarm of aircraft included a variety of highly capable warplanes. It also included support aircraft, some of which were rather unusual.

On the first night of the air war, the Iraqis claimed to down many coalition aircraft. But these "kills" were not what they appeared to be. In fact, they were decoys and drones—small pilotless aircraft. Drones could be operated by remote control, while decoys merely flew in a straight line until they ran out of fuel and went down. Both were designed to reflect radar beams in a

---

Coalition Pilots Face Iraqi Defenses

During the air war, coalition aircraft suffered remarkably few casualties. With its thick air defenses and modern fighters, Iraq still only managed to shoot down a handful of coalition planes. Looking back on the air war, it all seems very simple. But it did not seem either simple or safe to the pilots during combat. From a pilot's vantage point, the walls of fire created by Iraqi defenses appeared deadly, especially on the first night, before coalition attacks began to take their deadly toll on Iraqi defenders.

On the first night, television cameras from CNN were in Baghdad, broadcasting dramatic footage of a city lit up by tracers, flak, and vast antiaircraft gunfire. Although the Iraqis could not detect the Nighthawks on radar, they knew they were there, and they unloaded with their air-defense batteries. Even though they were firing blind, the Iraqis hoped that if they poured enough fire into the air, attacking jets would fly into it.

The F-117s flew high over the city, out of the range of the heavy fire from the ground and invisible to antiaircraft missiles. Nevertheless, with the sky ablaze from the air-defense guns, it was a terrifying sight for the pilots of the ten attacking F-117As. Rick Atkinson describes it in his book *Crusade: The Untold Story of the Persian Gulf War.*

> In vivid fountains of red and orange and gold, the enemy fire boiled up with an intensity that initially mesmerized more than it frightened. Missiles corkscrewed skyward or streaked up on white tubes of flame. Anti-aircraft rounds— 57mm, then 100mm—burst into hundreds of black and gray blossoms. Scarlet threads of

gunfire stitched the air, woven so thickly as to suggest a solid sheet of fire.

One pilot said the antiaircraft artillery fire was so thick that it appeared as if a man could walk on it. Some of the pilots doubted that all of the Nighthawks would complete their missions and return safely to Saudi Arabia. That same night, an F-111 attacking a suspected chemical-weapons storage shelter in Iraq encountered similarly heavy fire. In their book *The Generals' War: The Inside Story of the Conflict in the Gulf,* Michael R. Gordon and Bernard Trainor compare dodging that fire to "running through a shower without getting wet."

Iraqi antiaircraft guns respond to U.S. and British air strikes in Baghdad.

---

way that would make them resemble larger fighter aircraft. By preceding coalition attack jets, the decoys and drones would lure the Iraqis into turning on radar systems and firing SAMs and antiaircraft guns, thus helping the attackers avoid defenses or find and destroy them.

Air Superiority Aircraft

No country in the world could claim better attack aircraft than the United States. Four fighters were outstanding: the air force's F-16 Falcon and F-15 Eagle and the navy's F-14 Tomcat and F/A-18 Hornet. The air force fighters flew from bases in Saudi Arabia and Turkey. Tomcats and Hornets were flown from the six American aircraft carriers deployed in the Persian Gulf and Red Sea.

These four fighters all boasted great speed (as much as Mach 3, or three times the speed of sound) and maneuverability, making them deadly in air combat. Additionally, they bristled with sophisticated missiles for both air-to-air combat and ground attack missions (except for Tomcats, which were used almost exclusively to defend naval vessels). They all possessed advanced technology for flight control and for finding targets in the dark and in bad weather, making them lethal dangers to opponents. They were also equipped with electronic countermeasures against enemy radar and communications systems as well as defenses that helped them survive missile attacks. They could dispense hot flares

Able to fly at close to two times the speed of sound, an F/A-18 Hornet launches from the aircraft carrier USS Kitty Hawk *on January 21, 1991.*

to attract heat-seeking missiles and small clouds of chaff, pieces of aluminum or other material, to confuse radar units built into the surface-to-air or air-to-air missiles.

The fighters were used to seek out and engage Iraqi fighters and to escort and defend other coalition aircraft. The same aircraft that established coalition dominance of the skies also provided much of its punching power against targets on the ground. British and French fighters also flew strike missions. The British Tornado, which is similar to the F-14, was active in this role. The French Mirage 2000 also flew a small number of attack missions. In addition to the Hornet, the A-6 Intruder was the other important U.S. carrier-based attack plane. Because they carried a large payload, including precision-guided bombs, and can operate in all types of weather, the A-6 was the workhorse of carrier-based attack aircraft until it was retired several years after the war.

Electronic Warfare Planes

The striking power of attack aircraft and bombers was greatly magnified by companion aircraft specially designed for electronic warfare (EW). One EW plane, the EC-130H Compass Call, helped defend coalition aircraft by jamming enemy communications. By doing so, the Compass Calls hampered the ability of the Iraqis to attack coalition planes even when they could find them on radar since Iraqi early-warning radar crews could not inform air-defense gunners and fighters of the whereabouts of coalition attackers.

Most EW planes focused on radar itself. Their mission was to locate enemy radar and then to jam or confuse it. If Iraqi air defenses could not locate coalition warplanes, they stood very little chance of shooting them down. Like radio transmissions, radar beams can use many frequencies, and the Iraqis hoped their transmissions could be hidden in a thicket of frequency bands. But EW planes are designed to cover numerous frequency bands simultaneously. The EF-111 served in this role, as did the navy's carrier-based EA-6 Prowler. The F-4G Wild Weasel, a converted Vietnam-era fighter, was the most numerous of the radar-detecting planes.

In addition to jamming radar systems, these planes also destroyed radar sites. The electronic equipment of the radar hunters followed the radar beam back to its source, which would then be attacked by high-speed antiradar missiles (HARMs) launched from F-16s or the radar-detecting aircraft themselves.

The radar hunters and HARMs made it exceedingly dangerous for the Iraqis to turn on their radar systems. As two military experts note, "Turning on a SAM radar was like shining a flashlight in a dark room."[6] Thus, Iraqi soldiers manning antiaircraft installations faced a difficult dilemma. If they did not use radar, they had no chance of hitting the attackers and risked being wiped out without a fight. But if they turned on their radar to find the incoming coalition aircraft, they were inviting devastating attacks from HARMs. The coalition's ability to find and attack antiaircraft sites was of utmost importance since Iraq still had plenty of shoulder-fired SAMs and mobile antiaircraft guns even after the main components of their air-defense system were gone. In the campaign to destroy Iraqi air defenses, the United States and its allies used approximately one thousand HARMs.

With their radar systems neutralized, the Iraqis had to resort to a tactic used by the Soviets. They would either guess the flight path of attackers or identify them visually and unleash massive antiaircraft fire in their path, hoping the attackers would fly into the wall of fire. This crude tactic seldom worked. It was not an efficient way of locating coalition aircraft, and even when

Aircraft Carriers

Aircraft carriers are the Goliaths of modern naval warfare, the principal weapon of sea control. Throughout modern naval history, great battles at sea took place between warships within sight of each other exchanging fire from big guns. Beginning with World War II that changed as decisive naval engagements came to be fought primarily with carrier-based aircraft operating at great distances.

Carriers enable forces to project power at vast distances, bringing targets hundreds of miles from the sea within range of strike aircraft operating from these huge floating air bases. The largest of these huge ships weighs more than ninety thousand tons and is staffed by a crew of five thousand. Carriers are the military luxury of large, rich nations. Carrier battle groups are enormously expensive, costing approximately $20 billion. The carriers alone cost about $4 billion each. In addition to the United States, only France, Britain, and Russia maintain a handful of carrier battle groups, and these fleets are much smaller than those of the United States.

In the war against Iraq, there were no large naval battles because the Iraqi navy was too small even to consider duels against American warships. Nonetheless, carrier-based patrol and strike aircraft performed the important task of protecting commercial and naval vessels. Most of the carriers' one hundred F-14 Tomcats were used to patrol the waters of the Red Sea and Persian Gulf against Iraqi air or naval threats.

Carrier-based aircraft also represented substantial power on the part of coalition navies. Six American aircraft carriers provided floating bases and launch platforms for nearly 600 warplanes involved in the air war against Iraq. These carriers dispatched strike, electronic warfare, and reconnaissance aircraft in more than eighteen thousand sorties against Iraqi forces. In addition to the Tomcats, the six carriers provided 134 F/A-18 Hornets and 50 A-6 Intruders for bombing missions against Iraq. Overall, carrier-based planes carried out about 20 percent of the combat missions against the Iraqis during Desert Storm.

If the United States had not had access to bases in Saudi Arabia, Turkey, and elsewhere, carrier-based aircraft would have played an even more critical role.

Carrier-based aircraft were used for about 20 percent of the combat missions in Desert Storm.

the wall of fire was put in the right place, coalition planes were usually able to fly over or around it. Thus, jamming radar undoubtedly saved the lives of countless coalition air crews.

Airborne Intelligence

Fighters and attack aircraft also had the vitally important support of air-control planes. The most capable of these was the E-3 airborne warning and control system (AWACS), a converted Boeing 707 passenger plane. Distinguished by the large striped radar dome mounted on the plane's fuselage, an AWACS could locate and track several hundred friendly and enemy planes at once, at a distance of up to 350 miles. As an airborne traffic cop, the AWACS could warn coalition aircraft of any threats in the air; af-

Converted from 707 passenger planes, E-3 airborne warning and control systems (AWACS) planes monitored air traffic and detected potential enemy aircraft.

ter locating enemy planes, the AWACS could direct coalition craft to them.

The AWACS played another critically important role. It was the job of the AWACS's to ensure that coalition aircraft did not attack each other. Hundreds of coalition aircraft from several different countries prowled the air simultaneously, and they did not always have the means to communicate with each other—especially when they were maintaining radio silence to avoid alerting the Iraqis of their presence and location. And visual identification for fighters sometimes flying at fifteen hundred miles per hour was impossible at anything but the closest range. When pilots could see other planes, they were already vulnerable to air-to-air missiles.

The Iraqis had a much more primitive version of the AWACS, called the Adnan. But they only had three Adnan planes, their crews were poorly trained, and in the air they were highly vulnerable to coalition fighters. Thus, in actual combat, the Iraqis had no airborne warning and control aircraft. American AWACS planes, on the other hand, were constantly in the air, keeping the skies almost totally transparent for coalition pilots. In part because of the AWACS, there was not a single case of coalition aircraft mistakenly attacking one another.

The coalition had other advanced technologies to prevent "friendly fire" in the air. Using devices called IFF (identification, friend or foe), coalition aircraft sent out signals that identified themselves as friendly to other coalition aircraft. Planes that did not respond to IFF signals were usually presumed to be Iraqi ones. Some coalition aircraft were equipped with an even more sophisticated technology that allowed them to identify engine type by radar. Once they had the engine's signature, they could quickly match it up against lists of coalition and enemy engines, establishing another plane's identity.

The Coalition Achieves Air Control

Within the first twenty-four hours, Iraq's air-defense system was in complete shambles. The major command centers and subcenters were destroyed. The electrical system supporting Iraqi command and control had been severely damaged. Without these systems Iraq's high-altitude SAMs were ineffective. From the first night on, coalition aircraft could safely operate at fifteen thousand feet and above. At lower levels, Iraqi mobile SAMs and antiaircraft artillery fire continued to be a threat, but a manageable one. Some missions had to be aborted when pilots were confronted with heavy fire from antiaircraft artillery and SAMs. Nonetheless, the opening strikes were resoundingly successful, and events went much better than expected. Saddam Hussein was so angry over the catastrophic failure of the air-defense system that he ordered the execution of the air-defense chief. In fact, Hussein reportedly shot the man himself.

The opening strikes not only crippled Iraqi command and control and air defenses but also did much to neutralize threats posed by the Iraqi air force. One American fighter, an FA-18 Hornet, was destroyed, probably by an Iraqi MiG-25 interceptor, but Iraq's victory in this air-to-air engagement was unusual. On the first night, there were eight other dogfights between Iraqi and coalition pilots. The Iraqis lost them all. Five MiG-29s and three F-1 Mirages were blasted from the air. American technological advantages, combined with vastly superior pilot training and the Iraqis' dependence on control centers (most of which were jammed or destroyed), made air-to-air combat a one-sided affair.

Over the next few days, a few Iraqi pilots made the fatal mistake of challenging coalition fighters. Many fighters were simply placed in concrete shelters, where they remained vulnerable to coalition strikes. Others fled to northern Iraq, away from the areas of concentrated attacks, or even to Iran, as Iraqi pilots tried to escape an agonizing choice: destruction by coalition fighters or execution by Iraq's military authorities for refusing to fight. Many were shot down by coalition fighters as they attempted to flee.

As a result, Iraq no longer had a usable air force. The coalition had firmly established air superiority, and for the next six weeks, it would be free to fly tens of thousands of sorties (missions) against Iraqi military targets.

Chapter 3

The Instruments of Airpower

he goals of the air war were confidently expressed by American air force commander Brigadier General Buster Glosson in a pledge to President Bush: "I can guarantee you that the Iraqis won't be able to feed, resupply, or move their army because I'll have all the bridges down and I'll take their resupply away from them. Over a period of time they will shrivel like a grape when the vine's been cut." Glosson admitted that airpower alone could not drive Iraq's army from Kuwait. But if given enough time, Glosson said, "I can guarantee him [the president] I'll destroy it in place."[7]

With its air force neutralized, its air defenses devastated, and its communications systems severely disrupted, there was little Iraq could do to prevent coalition aircraft and bombers from prowling the skies over Kuwait and Iraq. But it could hope to limit the damage from air strikes by moving and concealing its military assets and by trying to deceive coalition pilots into believing

that untouched targets had already been destroyed.

Iraq's Defenses: Mobility and Concealment

Against the numerous and superior combat aircraft of the United States and its partners, Iraqi troop and weapons concentrations, industries, government buildings, fuel and ammunition depots, electric power facilities, and military installations were all highly vulnerable. American spy satellites could easily find such targets, and since they were large and stationary, they could easily be located and hit.

Still, Iraq hoped to limit damage somewhat. Some important targets could be moved around, and this, of course, included Iraqi leaders themselves. Saddam Hussein and his top military and political aides were constantly on the move, routinely sleeping in different places every night. This made it almost impossible to bomb the leaders who were making the

Although Saddam Hussein could not compete with the coalition's airpower, he frustrated its efforts by relocating Iraq's weapons and military equipment.

critical decisions about the occupation of Kuwait and later about the war with the U.S.-led coalition.

Many weapons systems were mobile. Except for tanks buried in the sand, Iraq's armored forces were also mobile. Many of Iraq's long-range guns—howitzers and artillery—were towed. By being moved around, they could escape destruction. Most of Iraq's frightful Scud missiles were fired from mobile launchers, which proved difficult for coalition bombers to locate. Important components of Iraq's nuclear, chemical, and biological weapons programs could be moved around also. Even when research and production facilities were bombed, these programs were only slowed down because major elements had been moved to safety. Shoulder-fired anti-aircraft missiles were highly mobile and were, in any event, too small to be targeted except when they were actually being used.

Some of Iraq's military equipment could be concealed or protected. The Iraqis placed their best military equipment in concrete-reinforced shelters that offered some protection from bombs. Fighter planes were kept in small hangarlike structures made of concrete, called revetments. Some equipment was small enough to be stored in buildings. Since no spy satellite could see through a roof, and since Iraq had numerous large buildings, equipment concealed in this way would be safe as long as spy satellites did not catch the Iraqis in the act of transporting and storing it. Tanks buried in the sand with only turrets showing were also difficult to spot from the air. Likewise, Scud launchers were carried on the backs of ordinary-looking trucks.

Iraq also stored important military equipment near buildings and archaeological sites it assumed the coalition would not be willing to target. American leaders were somewhat shocked to see spy-satellite photographs showing planes and tanks parked next to mosques, schools, and hospitals.

They were also angered at an Iraqi leadership willing to use its own people as shields and hostages against coalition bombs.

Deception

Iraq also hoped to limit bomb damage by offering the coalition fake targets and by deceiving coalition aircraft into thinking that untouched targets had already been bombed. When the air war began, the Iraqis painted the roofs of buildings that were likely targets so they would appear, from the air, as if they had already been bombed. In some places they started fires or scattered debris around possible military targets for the same purpose. If coalition bomber pilots believed that a target had already been hit, they might leave it alone.

The Iraqis also created dummy weapons. Phony planes and tanks were fashioned out of wood, sheets of metal, and other simple materials. Large pipes were stuck into the ground at angles, making them look like buried tanks. On the ground, these crude constructions could

Iraqis buried many tanks in the sand to make them difficult to see from the air.

not fool anyone. From fifteen thousand feet above, however, they looked very much like actual weapons. Ordnance wasted on dummy targets obviously could not be used to destroy real Iraqi weapons, and phony kills would give the coalition a distorted view of the effectiveness of bombing.

Weapons of the Air Campaign

Mobility, concealment, and deception did offer the Iraqis some protection from the full effects of the air war. Those weapons placed near schools, mosques, and archaeological sites were left alone. Some important buildings were left untouched because of bomb "damage" painted on their roofs. Likewise, mobility and concealment, plus the sheer number of possible targets, ensured that a large portion of Iraqi weapons and equipment were beyond the reach of coalition bombs.

Unfortunately for Iraq, these techniques could not spare its forces from savage punishment. Most weapons and equipment could not be concealed, and mobility did not always afford protection from strikes. Aided by patrol aircraft and spy satellites, the coalition sent fighters and bombers ranging over Kuwait and Iraq looking for targets of opportunity. With hundreds of attack aircraft aiding in the search for Iraqi military forces, even tanks on the move posed little challenge for the Coalition's modern attack aircraft.

Every day during the six-week air campaign, coalition headquarters in Saudi Arabia dispatched thousands of air tasking orders (ATOs), filling several thick volumes, allocating targets or target areas to individual warplanes. Reconnaissance aircraft and satellites provided damage assessment to determine if additional sorties were needed against particular targets. It was a large and highly complex operation designed to systematically degrade Iraqi forces. Carrying out the ATOs, coalition warplanes were well suited to the mission of making Iraq's occupation force in Kuwait shrivel like grapes on a cut vine and destroying that force in place.

Attack Aircraft and Bombers

The same aircraft that crippled Iraqi command control, communications, and intelligence, also known as C³I, and established coalition air superiority also played a key role in attacking Iraqi military targets throughout the air campaign. More than seven hundred American F-14s, F-15s, F-18s, and A-6s, as well as the French Mirage and British Tornado, were used in attack missions against Iraqi forces. Typically carrying seven thousand to twelve thousand pounds of bombs, rockets, and air-to-surface missiles, and often flying two or more missions per day, these planes were devastatingly effective against the virtually defenseless Iraqis.

U.S. bombers played an important role in the air war. The biggest role was played by America's massive strategic bomber the B-52 Stratofortress. B-52s operated in groups to saturate target areas with bombs. Though developed in the 1950s to carry

The B-52 Stratofortress played an important role in the air war against Iraq. Operating in groups, the B-52s dropped cluster bombs that scattered hundreds of bomblets over wide areas.

nuclear weapons, the B-52 had been used to drop conventional bombs since the Vietnam War. B-52s are neither fast nor agile, though they can use electronic countermeasures to protect themselves against enemy aircraft. They can fly great distances; flying nonstop from the United States, Stratofortresses could easily reach targets in Iraq.

B-52s carry a huge payload. A single plane can drop about fifty five-hundred-pound bombs or twenty two-thousand-pounders in a mission. Against Iraq, the B-52s often dropped cluster bombs, bombs with exploding canisters that scattered hundreds of bomblets over a wide area. As in Vietnam, B-52 bombers used cluster munitions to carpet bomb an area the size of several football fields in the shape of long, narrow rectangles, creating small craters every few feet. Carpet bombing was used to disable airfields and to attack large, soft (easy-to-destroy) targets such as military installations or large concentrations of military vehicles. The deafening roar of tens of thousands of pounds of munitions dropped from B-52s had a terrifying effect on those who survived the attacks. Many Iraqis who experienced just one such attack decided they had seen enough of America's airpower and surrendered.

Another bomber, the medium-range F-111, was also active in the air campaign. Equipped with forward-looking infrared radar and advanced avionics (the electronic systems that control navigation, steering, and other aspects of flight control), and able to fly at Mach 2, the F-111 is a highly capable aircraft. It has a combat radius of more than thirteen hundred miles, and can operate from a height of more than ten miles. It can carry thirty thousand pounds of ordnance, and it can deploy smart weapons. Thus, it was also well suited for bombing missions. Sixty-seven F-111s flew a total of twenty-five hundred sorties and accounted for some 2,200 kills, including 920 Iraqi tanks.

Bombs

Desert Storm is thought of as a high-tech war. One of the most striking symbols of this high-tech war is the laser-guided bomb obliterating targets with devastating accuracy. In reality, only 15 percent of the bombs dropped by the coalition were precision-guided munitions (PGMs), also called smart bombs. Most coalition bombs were old-fashioned gravity-controlled dumb bombs—that is, bombs that had no mechanisms for guiding them to the targets after being released from the planes.

But munitions were selected with care. Dumb bombs were used against big, soft targets such as buildings, weapon and supply depots, runways, and concentrations of troops. Moreover, even dumb bombs could be quite accurate. Advanced bombsights and computers made targeting calculations based on speed and altitude of the plane, wind speed, air pressure, and precise distance to the target so these bombs could be used with much greater precision than in earlier wars.

Sixty-seven F-111 bombers were sent to the Persian Gulf, flying a total of twenty-five hundred sorties.

Laser-guided bombs (pictured) allow targets to be hit with incredible precision.

PGMs employ a variety of technologies to guide their flight paths after release, sometimes right up to the point of impact. The guidance technologies can place warheads within a few feet of their aim points. The most frequently used PGMs in Desert Storm were laser-guided ones. The attacking plane, a companion aircraft, or even a spotter on the ground would point a laser beam at the target. A laser-seeker in the warhead would fix on the target, and computer-aided fins directed the falling bomb to the target. For greatest accuracy and against moving targets, the laser beam must "paint" the target until the bomb makes impact. When this is impossible because of dangers from antiaircraft fire or because of moving clouds or smoke, the warhead simply zeroes in on the place where the laser beam had pointed.

Some PGMs are equipped with television cameras in the nose cone. The image is either relayed to a weapons officer in the attacking plane or matched against images stored in an onboard computer. In either case, once a target is located, the bomb's guidance system locks onto the target and directs the bomb to it. Attack planes and PGMs also make use of heat-seeking sensors and radar. Thus, targets can be found and hit at night, in bad weather, and through the smoke of battle. In some cases, precision-guidance technologies are used in combination.

Stocks of smart munitions were low and had to be saved for the most important targets. Though in relatively short supply, these bombs contributed heavily to the success of the air campaign. Precision-guided munitions were the bombs of choice for small targets such as tanks and bridges, or for targeting weapons protected by concrete shelters. In past wars, such targets had either been impossible to hit or had required hundreds of bombing sorties. Smart bombs de-stroyed many of the tanks buried in the sand by the Iraqis. PGMs were also used against buildings, such as command headquarters in Baghdad and elsewhere, in order to avoid damage to nearby buildings and civilians. In the case of hardened (protected) buildings, only PGMs could provide the accuracy to hit the few small vulnerable areas, such as ventilation shafts, that would result in heavy damage.

Both smart and dumb bombs came in a range of sizes, most between five hundred and five thousand pounds. Naturally,

Bunker-Busters and Other Big Bombs

Bunkers had long presented special problems to bombers. Buried in the ground and heavily reinforced, bunkers protected their inhabitants from all but direct hits. In Iraq, bunkers protected the nation's political and military leaders. Since those leaders were responsible for the aggression against Kuwait and were directing the armed forces opposing the U.S.-led coalition, coalition leaders saw them as legitimate targets. At the least, the coalition wanted to put those bunkers at risk so that Iraqi leaders would be forced to move around frequently, disrupting Iraqi command operations and forcing leaders to use unreliable and insecure communications facilities.

Nuclear weapons could have served this mission, but there were strong moral and political arguments against their use. The U.S. Air Force did have one nonnuclear weapon that could perform the mission, a monster bomb called a fuel-air explosive. As the bomb neared the ground, it sent out a fine spray of fuel over a large area. The large fuel mist exploded in the air, creating a powerful concussion or shock wave over a large area. The ferocious explosion of a fuel-air explosive has been compared to the blast of a small nuclear weapon.

In addition to the antibunker mission, fuel-air explosives were used to kill concentrations of Iraqi soldiers in less-protected bunkers. They were also used against minefields, where their large blast would detonate most mines. The biggest drawback to this fearsome weapon was reliability; only about half of the fuel-air bombs that were dropped actually detonated.

Besides being unreliable, fuel-air explosives were not ideally suited for attacks on deep, heavily fortified bunkers. So during Desert Storm the U.S. Department of Defense ordered the rapid development of bombs capable of burrowing deeply and destroying well-fortified bunkers. One, the GBU-28, was a five-thousand-pound laser-guided bomb. Tests demonstrated that this bomb could penetrate over twenty feet of concrete or more than one hundred feet of earth.

For attacks on troops and minefields, the coalition also used a fifteen-thousand-pound bomb called the Daisy Cutter. The awesome concussion from the Daisy Cutter would kill all unprotected soldiers within a two-mile radius. Eleven of these fearsome weapons were dropped from specially equipped C-130s.

attack planes could carry more of the smaller bombs, for use against soft targets. Larger bombs were used against large targets and those that were hardened. Even larger bombs—some specially designed— were used to attack Iraqi troop concentrations and the underground bunkers of Iraqi leaders. Thus, the U.S. inventory of bombs was suited for a range of needs in the air war. In conjunction with air-to-surface missiles and unguided rockets, bombs enabled coalition forces to severely degrade Iraqi C^{3}I systems and military forces as well as the supplies that sustained them.

Tank Killers: Warthogs and Apaches

Several American aircraft were specially designed to support troops on the ground. The most important were an air force attack jet called the A-10 Thunderbolt and an army helicopter gunship, the Apache. The Cobra, another attack helicopter, which was developed ten years earlier and was used by the marines, had similar features and was also important. These aircraft were highly successful at destroying Iraq's premier instrument of ground warfare, tanks.

A slow, bulky, even ugly plane, the A-10 is known more commonly (yet affectionately) as the Warthog. Attractive or not, the Warthog was highly effective during Desert Storm. Flying at 300 miles per hour, the A-10s were much slower than fighters such as the F-15 and F-16. But because they lingered longer over the battle area, they could get a better look at their targets and spend more time pounding them. Highly maneuverable, the A-10 could attack, turn sharply and quickly make another pass over the battle area. Operating after the main air-defense weapons had been destroyed, the sturdy A-10 could swoop low for its attack, often taking numerous hits from lighter weapons. Though many suffered damage, few were actually shot down.

Warthogs were equipped with deadly armament, which usually included rockets, Maverick missiles, and a thirty-millimeter cannon. The Mavericks used infrared guidance systems to zero in on the heat of their targets (also allowing the A-10s to operate at night). Their cannon could chew up a battlefield, firing four thousand of the thirty-millimeter, depleted-uranium rounds per minute. Each of these oversize bullets is about eight inches long and an inch wide. Because they are much heavier than steel, the nonradioactive slugs are well suited to penetrate armor. Although low-tech planes (equipped with high-tech weapons), A-10s played a key role in destroying Iraqi tanks and other armored vehicles.

Apache helicopter gunships, often working in concert with A-10s, also participated in many tank-killing operations. Flying just above ground level, Apaches took advantage of dunes and small hills to remain unseen until they were right on top of Iraqi positions. Even flying low, the Apaches could find their targets by using the sophisticated forward-looking infrared

radar. The Apaches would suddenly rise up, bringing Iraqi tanks into their sights. Like A-10s, Apaches could saturate their targets with 30-millimeter cannon. Apaches could also destroy tanks from almost four miles away, outside the range of most Iraqi antiaircraft guns, by firing Hellfire missiles. Like Mavericks, Hellfires use heat-seeking sensors and lasers to lock onto targets. The 260 Apaches used in Desert Storm killed some 500 tanks, 120 armored vehicles, and assorted planes, helicopters, and radar installations.

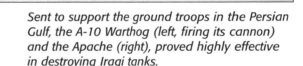

Sent to support the ground troops in the Persian Gulf, the A-10 Warthog (left, firing its cannon) and the Apache (right), proved highly effective in destroying Iraqi tanks.

Tankers

Though much better able to operate on their own than Iraqi fighters, coalition combat aircraft had considerable support. A fleet of aerial tankers, which kept the aircraft fueled and capable of operating over great ranges, was essential in the support role. Most of the tankers in the American fleet were put to work: four hundred in the United States and at U.S. bases worldwide and three hundred directly deployed to the Persian Gulf region. The KC-135 was the main tanker. A converted Boeing 707, the KC-135 carried sixty tons of fuel that could be delivered to combat aircraft while in flight. In addition to the two hundred KC-135s sent to the region, the United States provided another fifty KC-10s (a converted MD-10 commercial aircraft carrying ninety tons of fuel) and a handful of smaller-capacity KC-130s and KA-6Ds.

Tankers were the workhorses that kept other coalition aircraft in the air. Midair refueling by tankers got fighters and bombers to the Gulf in the first place. For instance, to fly the sixty-five hundred miles from the United States to Saudi Arabia, an F-15 needed eighty-five thousand pounds of fuel, delivered in seven separate midair refuelings. In the opening hours of the air strikes, 160 tankers and command aircraft took to the skies to support 400 combat planes. With tanker support, fighters and bombers could operate from a large system of bases, some located a long distance from the Persian Gulf. With aerial refueling, strike aircraft could hit targets deeper inside Iraq or spend more time searching for targets, and they could carry bigger loads of bombs and missiles.

The Effectiveness of Weapons in the Air Campaign

After crippling Iraq's air defenses, coalition warplanes spent six weeks pounding Iraqi forces and military support systems. Altogether, the Coalition's military aircraft flew more than one hundred thousand missions. Of these, more than thirty thousand were strike sorties. The impact of the bombing campaign was much greater than in previous wars because the coalition faced only minimal air defenses and because technology allowed for tremendous accuracy in bombing.

Military forces cannot fight in an organized and effective manner without leadership. Iraq's leaders were hard to find, and they did have a system of secure bunkers. Nonetheless, attacks on those bunkers kept them off balance and in fear. Additionally, by destroying those facilities best suited for military communications, the coalition forced the Iraqis to use other facilities with less-secure communications, which were often intercepted by satellites and spy planes, giving the coalition an intelligence bonanza.

Direct attacks on the command, control, and communications systems were more effective than strikes aimed at the leadership. Coalition warplanes struck television and radio transmitters, receiving stations, and microwave towers to disrupt or eliminate over-the-air communications between Iraq's military forces and their leaders. Iraq's civilian telephone network handled more than half of the military communications transmitted by wire, so telecommunications systems were also hit hard. Despite Iraq's efforts to repair damage and to create multiple lines of communication, the coalition's overall effort was quite successful. Leaders in Baghdad were often completely in the dark about military developments in the Kuwaiti theater of operations, and Iraqi commanders in the field were frequently unable to make requests or receive orders from Baghdad.

The air attacks interrupted Iraqi supply lines as well as communications. Armies are great hungry beasts, which march on their stomachs, as Napoléon once said. In fact, armies must be supplied with much more than food. They also have immense needs for water, medicine, weapons, ammunition, spare parts, and other supplies. An army that cannot meet these enormous needs is an army in deep trouble. By going after both production and storage facilities in Iraq and supplies moving from Iraq to Kuwait, coalition airpower ensured that Iraq had immense problems meeting those needs.

Production facilities for Iraq's smaller weapons and spare parts were located in Iraq itself, as were numerous supply depots of weapons. These important facilities were the targets of three thousand coalition missions. Many of these depots were so large (for example, one military supply complex covered an area of ten square miles) that even repeated strikes could only destroy a fraction of their stockpiles. Similarly, ammunition stocks at one storage facility were so large that B-52 strikes set off a huge explosion equivalent to an erupting volcano. Overall, approximately 30 percent of Iraq's conventional weapons production facilities were badly damaged or destroyed.

Modern armies also rely on huge quantities of fuel. The centers that produced and distributed the gas and oil that fueled Iraq's military equipment were also subjected to intense attacks. As a result, an already slow moving army became even less mobile since Iraq could not deliver the fuel needed by its tanks and other military equipment.

Just as production and storage facilities in Iraq were vulnerable, so were the troops and supplies as they were transported from Iraq to Kuwait. Whether moving by day or night, the trucks bringing supplies into Kuwait could be located by coalition patrol aircraft. Upon finding the supply trucks, the patrol planes would call in fighters. Within minutes, only burning shells would be left.

Iraq's resupply effort was even more vulnerable because only a handful of transportation links existed between Iraq and Kuwait, and those links were readily visible from the air. Maps, aerial surveillance, and spy satellites ensured that the coalition knew exactly where the roads and railroads were located. Precision-guided bombs enabled coalition aircraft to achieve a high success rate, even against targets that in previous wars would have been very hard to hit in strikes on supply routes. Of the fifty-four highway and railroad bridges on the routes between Iraq and Kuwait, only four were completely undamaged. Forty of those bridges were either destroyed or were severely damaged to the point of being unusable.

The effects were substantial. Frontline Iraqi troops were left with shortages of weapons, ammunition, and spare parts. Many of the Iraqis who surrendered lacked food and water. Medicine on the front lines was also scarce. Because of this, ordinary Iraqi soldiers knew that wounds that were ordinarily easy to treat could be fatal. And the danger of wounds was very real because

Iraqi forces represented the main targets for coalition air strikes.

Degrading Iraq's Military Forces

The air campaign took a heavy toll on Iraq's armed forces. By the beginning of the ground war (G day) on February 24, Iraq's air force was completely neutralized. Its naval ports and facilities suffered heavy damage, and almost all of its small navy was disabled or sunk. Iraq's occupying army in Kuwait was also hit hard, with its frontline forces taking the brunt of the Coalition's air strikes.

In many Iraqi divisions, the fear of death from the air and the reality of hunger and thirst led as many as half of the

Iraqi forces suffered substantial losses from the six weeks of bombing; the coalition left them with shortages of weapons, ammunition, food, water, and medicine.

troops to desert. In all, front-line Iraqi forces lost half their strength during the air campaign. During the Iran-Iraq War, Iraqi soldiers had slept in their armored personnel carriers and tanks at night, safe and secure from attacks by the lightly armed Iranian troops. In Kuwait, however, Iraqi soldiers came to see their armored vehicles as potential coffins. Even at night, death could arrive without warning as coalition warplanes with their terrifyingly accurate bombs suddenly swept overhead hunting for tanks and other targets of opportunity. Even the better-supplied Republican Guard divisions deployed far behind the front lines lost a quarter of their strength on average as a result of air strikes.

Altogether, the six-week air campaign wiped out approximately seventeen hundred of Iraq's forty-three hundred tanks, one thousand of its three thousand armored personnel carriers, and fifteen hundred of its three thousand artillery pieces. On the eve of the ground war, Iraq's occupation force in Kuwait was reeling but not destroyed. Entrenched Iraqi forces could still hope to impose heavy casualties on coalition ground forces. Additionally, both during and after the air campaign, Iraq had the potential to mount threats of its own on land and at sea.

Chapter 4

Checking Iraqi Threats on Land and at Sea

Despite their vulnerability to coalition airpower, the Iraqis had military cards to play. They could attack coalition troops with Scud missiles tipped with either chemical or high-explosive warheads. They could also attack Israel with Scud missiles, thereby pulling that nation into the war and likely breaking up the coalition. Likewise, they could attempt to take the war to sea, attacking naval vessels or commercial shipping in the Persian Gulf.

The United States bore most of the responsibility for meeting these threats. In response to the menace of chemical weapons, the United States had to ensure that troops took defensive measures, and it quietly made counterthreats. In response to the Scud danger the United States directed a large number of warplanes to search out and destroy Scuds and their launchers, and it deployed and used defensive, or antimissile, missiles, called Patriots, in Saudi Arabia and in Israel. Against

threats to the Gulf itself, the United States responded with a large naval deployment, which also augmented coalition firepower and threatened Iraq with an amphibious assault directed right at Kuwait City, the capital of Kuwait.

Scuds and Patriot Missiles

Iraq's threat to use Scud missiles was one of the coalition's biggest worries. These thirty-seven-foot-long missiles had a range of two hundred to four hundred miles. Iraq possessed Scud-B missiles, which it had acquired earlier from the Soviet Union, and their own upgraded version of the Scud. The Iraqi version had a longer range than the Soviet model, but it carried a smaller warhead since it had to carry more fuel. Neither version was very accurate. Thus, unlike American cruise missiles, the Scuds could not be used with precision against military targets. But they could be used against cities or against concentrations of troops or weapons. If fitted with warheads

Used in combat for the first time in Desert Storm, the Patriot missile was deployed to Israel for the defense against Iraq's Scud missiles.

carrying deadly nerve gas, the Scuds could cause dozens, even hundreds, of casualties.

In Washington, according to Michael R. Gordon and Bernard Trainor in their book *The Generals' War,* "no problem worried officials more than what might happen if Israel entered the war."[8] The Israelis, of course, were extremely alarmed by Saddam Hussein's threats to attack Israel with Scuds. The coalition did not have to wait long to find out whether Iraq would make good on its threat. On January 18, the second day of the war, Iraq launched eight Scud missiles against Israel, some of which hit apartment buildings. Nobody was killed, but forty-seven people were injured; likewise, four hundred apartments were destroyed and another twelve hundred were damaged. The Israelis waited tensely to see if the following round of Scuds would bring deadly chemical warheads into Israel's cities. The United States reacted immediately, ordering a massive effort to find and destroy the Scuds and rapidly deploying modernized Patriot air-defense missiles to Israel.

The Patriot was originally developed as an antiaircraft missile. Later, it was re-designed to shoot down ballistic missiles. Attempting to destroy a missile whizzing through the atmosphere at several thousand miles per hour is like trying to shoot a bullet with a bullet. To accomplish this mission, a Patriot does not actually have to hit its target. Radar directs it into the missile's

Hunting for Scuds

The great Scud hunt was a large-scale effort to find and destroy the Scud launchers from the air. The hunt was partially successful, but it also showed some of the limitations of airpower.

Twenty-eight of the Iraqi Scuds were on concrete launching pads at fixed sites. Because they could not be moved, the coalition easily located and destroyed them. But others launchers were highly mobile. The United States had the ability to locate Scud launches by using early-warning satellites designed to identify the launch of Soviet nuclear missiles by detecting the heat from their rocket engines. Iraq's Scuds had smaller engines than the large long-range Soviet missiles and thus produced less heat. For that reason, it took a longer time for the computers to determine that a missile had been launched.

By the time the data was analyzed and transmitted to the Persian Gulf and fighters were dispatched, it was usually too late because the Iraqis could "shoot and scoot." The trucks carrying the Scuds could be on their way five minutes after launching their missiles. Within ten minutes of launching, they could be five miles away. The semitrailer trucks carrying the mobile Scuds could not be easily identified since they looked the same as regular trucks used to transport goods. The large area and rugged terrain in western Iraq also made it fairly easy for the Iraqis to hide the Scud-launching trucks. Further, Iraq used decoys to confuse coalition aircraft, and many of the Scuds that were reported to have been destroyed turned out to be decoys.

With practice and adjustments, the warning time was shortened. Although there was just enough time to put Patriot missiles on ready alert, there still was not enough time to find and destroy the mobile launchers. Few mobile launchers were actually hit. Nonetheless, there were successes. After the Scud barrages of January 18 and 19, the coalition's Scud hunt quickly went into high gear. The launch areas had to be preprogrammed into the Scuds' computers so they could be aimed at their designated targets. In a matter of days, the coalition became familiar with the well-defined areas in which the mobile Scuds operated.

Coalition surveillance and attack aircraft intensively patrolled the launch areas in western Iraq looking for the first signs of movement by Scud-launching vehicles. F-16s and A-10s patrolled by day, and by night F-16s and F-15Es—equipped with special navigational and targeting radars—took up the hunt. They were joined by carrier-based A-6E Intruders equipped with forward-looking infrared radar. B-52s bombed suspected launch sites, and other planes dropped numerous area-denial mines, which are designed to keep enemy troops out of a given area. Special forces also operated in the Iraqi desert looking for Scud launchers. Because of all of these efforts, it became very difficult for the Iraqis to fire from their preprogrammed areas. The attacks quickly tapered off and soon ceased altogether.

path, and when the two missiles are close to each other, the Patriot warhead explodes. The attacking missile is destroyed or severely damaged when it flies through the cloud of exploding debris.

Patriots had destroyed missiles in tests, but controlled tests and actual combat are quite different. In tests, everything is known about the "attacking" missile—when and where it is going to be fired and its speed, trajectory, and altitude. In real combat, none of those facts are known. Furthermore, it is not enough just to destroy the missile. The warhead itself actually has to be destroyed or it might still explode and cause damage on the ground.

Desert Storm was the first combat test for the Patriot. Patriots have a short range, so they had to be located near the most likely Scud targets in Israel and Saudi Arabia. Altogether, the Iraqis fired approximately eighty Scuds at targets in those two countries. Few did any real damage. One, however, struck an American military barracks near Dhahran, Saudi Arabia, killing twenty-eight and wounding ninety-eight, the worst casualties of the war for the United States. A Patriot battery deployed there was temporarily out of commission.

The Patriot's effectiveness during the war was later questioned, causing much controversy. Initially, American officials claimed stunning successes for the Patriots. In some cases, incoming Scuds were seen blowing up in midair after the Patriots were fired. Upon closer examination, however, it became clear that the Patriots did not have such a high rate of success. A few critics even claimed that no Scuds were destroyed by Patriots.

Some Scuds managed to reach their targets even though two Patriot missiles had been fired at each Scud. In addition, some apparent "kills" might have been the result of design flaws in the Scuds, not interception by Patriots. In fact, the poor design of the Scuds actually offered protection against the Patriots. The Scuds often tumbled and disintegrated in midair, accidentally presenting the Patriots with multiple targets. In one instance, five attacking Scuds broke into fourteen pieces, drawing twenty-eight Patriots.

Whatever the reality about the Patriots' success, they made Israeli and coalition soldiers feel more secure. The sight and sound of a Patriot roaring into the night sky, its rocket engine emitting flame, were dramatic. When the firing of the Patriots was followed by an explosion and the sight of an incoming Scud bursting into dozens of small flaming pieces, observers on the ground readily believed that the Patriots were a great success.

As Patriots were rushed to Israel and Saudi Arabia for defense against Scud attacks, large numbers of coalition warplanes were ordered to hunt down and destroy Scuds. Strike aircraft were diverted from other missions for the hunt. In all, more than fourteen hundred strike missions were directed against Scud launchers and production facilities. Because mobile Scuds were hard to find and were not militarily significant, the army saw this as a poor way to use airpower. The army wanted as much of the air campaign as possible directed against Iraq's fortified forces in Kuwait, forces it would eventually have to fight.

Military arguments aside, Patriots and the Scud hunt achieved an important political goal by reassuring Israel, Saudi Arabia, and American troops. Even though Iraq fired forty-two Scuds at Israel, the Israeli government made the difficult decision to honor Washington's request to stay

A Patriot missile does not have to hit its target directly; once radar has directed the Patriot into the attacking missile's path, the Patriot warhead explodes, destroying the approaching missile.

out of the war. Iraq's fearsome wild-card weapon was neutralized.

Chemical Weapons

At the outset of war, Iraq was estimated to possess four hundred tons of mustard gas and nerve gas. Mustard gas causes skin blisters and potentially fatal lung damage when inhaled. Any form of exposure to nerve gas (a chemical weapon attacking the nervous system) can be fatal, even in minute amounts. Chemical weapons can be placed in the warheads of missiles, the shells of artillery, or bombs dropped from planes. After being fired or dropped, the canisters containing chemical agents explode, releasing poisonous clouds that fall to the earth.

The coalition's response to the threat of chemical attack took three forms: defensive, offensive, and deterrent. Patriot missiles constituted one defensive step. Another important defensive measure was equipping soldiers with gas masks and suits. Protective gear was especially important if Iraq used nerve gas since skin contact with even tiny amounts of nerve agents can be lethal. Though hot and uncomfortable, the suits allowed soldiers to operate safely near Iraqi forces, especially during the four-day ground offensive.

The coalition also acted offensively, attempting to seek out and destroy Iraq's chemical weapons as well as their delivery systems and the production facilities that made the weapons. While the great Scud hunt received a lot of attention, the early strikes that destroyed or scattered Iraq's air force eliminated the aircraft that are the most reliable and effective instruments for delivering chemical attacks.

Deterrence was also important. The Bush administration publicly kept open the possibility that the United States might respond with nuclear weapons if Iraq used chemical warfare. The American president also indicated that the coalition would forcibly remove Saddam Hussein's government from power if chemical weapons were used.

Apart from coalition policies, the Iraqis had serious command and control prob-

lems with their chemical arsenal. Additionally, leaky weapons and inadequate Iraqi protection equipment meant that there was a real danger that the Iraqis themselves might have been the biggest victims if they had attempted to use chemical weapons.

For whatever reasons, no chemical weapons were used. In all likelihood, the combination of Iraqi deficiencies plus coalition defensive and offensive efforts

Although the protective gear was hot and uncomfortable, coalition troops wore it in case of chemical warfare during the four-day ground offensive.

and deterrent threats eliminated the one weapon in the Iraqi arsenal that might have produced massive casualties on the coalition side.

Meeting Iraqi Threats to the Gulf

On land, the coalition had to cope with the threat of Scud attacks and chemical weapons. At sea, it had to prevent Iraq from disrupting commerce and threatening its naval forces.

Iraq's navy was tiny. Its biggest ship was a training frigate. Otherwise, the Iraqi navy did not boast large surface vessels that could match the power of American warships. Although Iraq lacked aircraft carriers, it did have the ability to threaten both merchant ships and coalition naval vessels in the Persian Gulf. It had ten missile attack boats and a number of fast patrol boats capable of firing antiship missiles. It also had three subchasers and a number of boats capable of sweeping or laying mines.

The coalition, on the other hand, was able to amass an impressive display of naval power. By the start of the war, the United States had 165 ships in the Persian Gulf, Red Sea, and eastern Mediterranean. Other coalition members provided an additional 65 ships. The armada included a variety of support vessels, such as hospital ships, supply ships, and repair ships. It also included small specialized vessels such as minesweepers. At the other end of the size spectrum, six immense nuclear-powered American aircraft carriers, carrying nearly six hundred combat aircraft, provided enormous punch-

ing power. Each carrier led a battle group consisting of two attack submarines, a number of large warships (destroyers, cruisers, and frigates), and several smaller support vessels. The submarines offered protection for the carrier group and conducted surveillance and intelligence missions.

Mines

Although it was small, the Iraqi navy was capable of making considerable mischief in the Persian Gulf. One threat that Iraq posed was a fairly primitive one: mines. Fortunately for the coalition, Iraq did not possess the most modern mines, which rest on the ocean floor and detonate after detecting sound, magnetic waves, or a change in water pressure from ships passing overhead. These modern mines are hard to detect and could have done considerable damage to shipping because the United States had not invested enough in modernizing its minesweeping forces.

Iraq did possess old-fashioned "contact" mines, which floated near the surface while being connected to the bottom by chains. Iraq managed to lay more than one thousand contact sea mines. As a result, two American ships were damaged by the exploding mines.

Many ships were equipped with a sensitive sonar system that enabled them to detect and avoid mines. The United States had five minesweeping ships (three old and two new ones), Britain deployed five, and Belgium and Saudi Arabia contributed a few more. The United States and Britain both

Finding Mines the Hard Way

Iraq's mines may have been fairly primitive, but there were a lot of them in the confined waters of the upper Gulf. The presence of so many mines was a source of anxiety for coalition sailors and their commanders. Even though no vessels were sunk by mines, two were damaged by mine detonations. One of them was the USS *Tripoli,* a helicopter carrier that was leading the antimine effort. The huge explosion tore a sixteen-by-twenty-six-foot hole in the hull. Although damage was lim-

ited, the incident was extremely frightening to the sailors on board and could have caused a naval catastrophe. Michael R. Gordon and Bernard Trainor, in their book *The Generals' War: The Inside Story of the Conflict in the Gulf,* describe what took place immediately after the blast:

> The engineers shut down the boiler to prevent an explosion. But one of the backup emergency diesel generators was flooded. There was no power in the forward part of the ship. Worse, the blast had ripped a hole in the tanks that carried the JP-fuel for the Sea Stallion helicopters and blown apart buckets of noxious gray paint in the main storage area. The entire forward part of the ship had filled up with explosive fuel and paint vapors. [Captain] McEwen was afraid that a spark could ignite the fumes with catastrophic consequences for the crew. The *Tripoli* had been sent to clear a path for others, but now all its energy was needed to save itself.

Fortunately, fast action by a highly skilled crew prevented a lethal explosion. The *Tripoli* and the other ship hit by a mine survived and were repaired in short order. Mines claimed no other casualties.

An Iraqi mine tore a sixteen-by-twenty-six-foot hole in the hull of the USS Tripoli, *a helicopter carrier deployed in the Persian Gulf.*

had minesweeping helicopters that used sonar and hydrofoil sleds that mimicked the sounds and magnetic fields of ships to locate mines. Helicopters also pulled long metal blades through the water to cut the tethers holding mines beneath the surface. After floating to the surface, the mines could be destroyed easily with guns or explosives. Warplanes also sought out and sank the Iraqi trawlers that were laying the mines.

There were shortcomings, though. Even against primitive mines, the navy was not entirely confident that well-swept areas were really free of mines. The immediate coastal area was not swept, which was one reason why coalition commanders decided not to mount an amphibious invasion of Kuwait. General Norman Schwarzkopf, the coalitions' military commander, complained that the navy minesweeping force was "old, slow, ineffective, and incapable of doing the job."[9]

Overall, however, the minesweeping operation was a success. Despite doubts and the inability to sweep the mines that were closest to the coast, the coalition prevented Iraq from disrupting shipping and from causing significant damage to naval vessels. Thus, another Iraqi threat was neutralized fairly easily by superior coalition forces.

Threats from Iraqi Forces on Islands and Drilling Platforms

Iraq had many oil-drilling platforms and small islands in the Persian Gulf. These, too, posed a military threat. For a country without large warships, they were excellent platforms for antiaircraft and antiship missiles. Because they were located on routes used by carrier-based coalition aircraft, they were also highly useful as forward observation posts for the information-poor Iraqis. Iraqi observers could simply sight the planes and, by noting the time and direction taken by the aircraft, make educated guesses about where those planes were heading. Using radios, the observers would warn their countrymen, who would then ready their antiaircraft guns and missiles. U.S. pilots knew that this simple tactic could be deadly effective, as was the case in Vietnam when many American planes were shot down after observers passed along warnings to air-defense forces.

Consequently, naval forces were quickly called on to neutralize this threat. Frigates, helicopters, and planes bombarded the islands and oil rigs, and helicopter assault teams attacked many of them, forcing Iraqi troops to surrender. In some cases, the marines and navy sea, air, land (SEAL)s, commandos who took the platforms and islands, discovered caches of shoulder-fired antiaircraft missiles. The assaults on islands and oil rigs sometimes involved short but fierce firefights. The Americans' rapid and overwhelming successes again demonstrated the importance of superior training and equipment.

The Missile Threat

At the beginning of the war, Iraq had twenty-five SU-24 attack planes (which are

The Chinese Silkworm was an antiship missile used unsuccessfully by the Iraqi forces.

similar to American F-111s) that could threaten ships with an assortment of bombs, rockets, and air-to-surface missiles. The greatest danger to ships in the Gulf came from Iraqi missiles. Iraq possessed several types of modern antiship missiles. One was the Chinese Silkworm. Iraq's fifty land-based Silkworms threatened ships at a distance of about seventy miles. Its four long-range B-6D bombers could also carry Silkworms. There were two close calls with Silkworms, but sophisticated defense systems prevailed in both cases. One Silkworm landed near the U.S. battleship *Missouri*. The Silkworm's radar may have been deceived by countermeasures. A sec-

ond Silkworm was on target to hit a British warship, the HMS *Gloucester*, but it was destroyed in midair by two Sea Dart surface-to-air missiles fired by the *Gloucester*.

In addition to Silkworms, Iraq's other major antiship missile was the French Exocet. Exocets could reach targets between forty and a hundred miles away and could be fired from Iraq's French-made Super Frelon helicopters or from its thirty-two F-1 fighters. They could also be launched from six of Iraq's thirteen missile boats. (The other seven missile boats carried the Soviet-made Styx missile.) Even small but fast patrol boats could be outfitted to launch Exocets. Skimming the surface of the sea, the fifteen-foot-long Exocet was extremely hard to detect on radar. Moving at almost the speed of sound, it could reach its target quickly. Coalition planners knew that the battle-tested capabilities of the Exocet had to be respected.

Thus, even though Iraq's navy was small, the coalition had to take Iraqi threats at sea seriously, especially in the shallow and confined waters of the Persian Gulf, which in previous years had been deemed unsafe for large American naval vessels. The coalition's larger ships (mostly American ones), consisting of destroyers, cruisers, and frigates, primarily served defensive missions, protecting the carriers and other ships from attacks from the sea or air. Measuring from 450 to 600 feet and carrying crews of about four hundred, these four-thousand- to ten-thousand-ton ships were equipped with Harpoon antiship missiles, torpedoes, antisubmarine rockets, several types of antiaircraft missiles, and large-shell, rapid-fire Phalanx antiaircraft guns. Additionally, some carried a handful of helicopters. Aegis-class destroyers and cruisers bristled with sophisticated radar systems to provide long-range warning of approaching planes or ships and short-range missile-tracking capability.

Throughout the conflict, U.S. carrier-based aircraft continued to guard against any remaining threat to coalition ships from Iraqi aircraft or ships. The coalition used several different types of aircraft working in teams to find and attack Iraqi ships capable of firing antiship missiles. Two sophisticated reconnaissance aircraft had the primary responsibility for finding Iraq's small ships, the British Nimrod (which is similar to a U.S. AWACS plane) and the American carrier-based P-3C Orions. Several types of helicopters, which were equipped with antiship missiles and guns, took part in the operations, as did a variety of fighter and attack aircraft. Additionally, attack aircraft bombed any Iraqi naval vessel they could find in port.

The naval forces' defensive mission was greatly aided by the effort early in the air campaign to scatter or destroy Iraqi fighters, which succeeded in removing Iraq's best platforms for launching antiship missiles. One by one, Iraq's ships were hunted by groups of coalition aircraft. The single biggest engagement occurred on January 30 near the small island of Būbiyān. The Battle of Būbiyān lasted for thirteen hours. In thirteen separate engagements, coalition aircraft sank Iraqi vessels or forced them to flee to Iran. By February 2, every one of Iraq's missile boats was sunk or disabled. When the land war began three weeks later, 143 of Iraq's 165 naval vessels had been destroyed or severely damaged by the coalition's carrier-based air forces. Iraq's navy was virtually destroyed, and its naval threat was completely eliminated. As with other aspects of the war, Iraqi forces were simply outclassed by the numerous, diverse, and technologically superior forces deployed by the U.S.-led coalition.

In addition to providing defense against direct Iraqi threats, coalition naval forces ensured that Iraq was not able to augment its strength by violating the international embargo on its imports and exports.

Enforcing the Embargo

Immediately after Iraq invaded Kuwait, the United States went to work to get the members of the UN Security Council to agree to an economic embargo of Iraq to weaken and isolate the country. At the outset, Washington hoped that the embargo would drive Iraq from Kuwait. It did not, but it was nonetheless an important military measure in the coalition's campaign to degrade Iraq's military capabilities.

Although the Security Council resolution imposed a strict embargo, it was not self-enforcing. It required muscle, a military presence to prevent cheating by countries that could profit from selling goods to Iraq or by buying its oil. Naval forces from the United States and other coalition countries provided that muscle. Enforcement was most needed at sea, where the majority of illegal commerce was conducted. Overall, coalition naval vessels stopped nearly eight thousand merchant ships. Of those, roughly one thousand were boarded and inspected. By inspecting the merchant ships, the United States and its partners ensured that cargo ships were carrying what they said they were carrying. While any

cargo might be destined for Iraq, some cargoes were more suspicious than others. Approximately seventy merchant ships were turned away because coalition naval crews concluded that they were trying to sneak goods into Iraq. The mere presence of coalition naval vessels discouraged most from attempting to defy the embargo. As a result, the embargo-enforcement mission was a success.

Iraq's Counterthreats Neutralized

Iraq's ability to mount counterthreats on land and at sea were simply stymied by the abundance and sophistication of coalition military resources. The combination of defensive measures, offensive operations, and deterrent threats negated Iraq's threat to use chemical weapons. Patriot missiles, an aggressive Scud hunt, some luck, and the defects of the Scuds themselves enabled the coalition to manage the missile threat, despite the limited success of strikes against Israel and against U.S. forces in Dhahran.

Coalition naval forces, including sea-based airpower, prevented Iraq from widening the war to the waters of the Persian Gulf. They enforced the embargo, which did much to weaken Iraq. As Norman Friedman, a prominent naval analyst, concludes, "Sea power tends to act invisibly but powerfully."[10] In addition to performing defensive missions, naval forces facilitated offensive operations by the coalition by providing the sealift that brought overwhelming ground forces to the Kuwaiti theater of operations, by augmenting land-based airpower for the

The Embargo

There were political and military purposes behind the embargo imposed on Iraq shortly after it invaded Kuwait. The United States and other backers of the embargo considered it very important politically. The embargo was a form of punishment intended to show just how outraged the world community was over Iraq's aggression. The embargo dramatically showed how isolated Iraq was, which in turn made it more difficult politically for countries to support Iraq or oppose the United States and other countries taking action against Iraq.

The embargo was also important militarily. By cutting off Iraq's imports, the embargo made it difficult for Iraq to get needed goods from outside. The country would not be able to purchase weapons or spare parts for the military equipment it already had. Iraq would not be able to purchase food, medicine, or other goods needed by both the army and the civilian economy. This, too, would damage Iraq's war-making capabilities. Additionally, any strains on the civilian economy might intensify opposition within Iraq to Saddam Hussein's policies. If inconvenience and suffering within the civilian population were great enough, Saddam's government might be overthrown—or so hoped the United States and its allies.

The embargo also applied to Iraq's exports, the goods it sold to other countries. Iraq's main export was oil. By preventing Iraq from selling oil, the embargo deprived Hussein's regime of its principal source of revenues. Without the large income from oil sales, it would be difficult for the Iraqi government to purchase necessities from producers inside Iraq or to use the lure of high prices to get other foreign producers to defy the embargo by secretly selling Iraq goods. Without oil income, it would be difficult to pay government employees, including the army. Unpaid soldiers were not likely to fight very hard and might even overthrow the government.

The Bush administration and the U.S. Congress hoped that the embargo would make military action unnecessary. If the embargo proved greatly damaging to the Iraqi economy, Hussein might decide to pull out of Kuwait. The embargo was, in fact, very painful for the Iraqis. Yet despite the serious damage to the economy, the Iraqi government refused to give up Kuwait. When the UN's January 15 deadline neared, General Colin Powell (chairman of the Joint Chiefs of Staff) and many members of Congress favored a delay in the start of military operations in the hope that the embargo would eventually force Iraq out of Kuwait. Fearing that wind and heat would make combat difficult in the spring, President Bush was not willing to wait. The embargo had weakened Iraq, but the only way to liberate Kuwait would be by force.

air war against Iraq, by bombarding Iraqi coastal positions and carrying out key strategic strikes with Tomahawk missiles, and by tying down Iraqi forces along the coast with the threat of amphibious assault. Thus, even if air forces delivered most of the devastating blows that left Iraqi forces reeling in the course of six weeks, naval forces added significant force to the vise grip that crushed Iraq's occupation force in Kuwait. But it was the ground forces that delivered the knockout blow.

Chapter 5

The War on the Ground

The threat of chemical weapons came to nothing, and the Iraqis were checked at sea. Meanwhile, the air war was devastatingly effective. But airpower alone could not compel Saddam Hussein to give up Kuwait unless the coalition was willing to target Iraq's population centers. For both moral and political reasons, this was unthinkable. Ground forces were needed to secure the final victory.

Iraq's Defensive Challenge

Saddam Hussein boasted that in the event of a ground war, the coalition would face the greatest of all battles. Hussein could only hope that his dug-in troops, backed by the elite Republican Guard, could offer enough resistance to inflict heavy casualties on coalition forces, forcing them to retreat.

The most obvious place for the coalition to attack the Iraqi occupation force in Kuwait would be straight up from Saudi Arabia since most its ground forces were deployed there. Consequently, Iraqi defensive efforts were concentrated along that 140-mile border. To cover this extensive border region, Iraq deployed most of its divisions, heavily armed with tanks, artillery, and antiaircraft batteries. Once in place, these forces hunkered down. Authors Lawrence Freedman and Efraim Karsh describe some of the defensive preparations in their book *The Gulf Conflict, 1990–1991:*

> Minefields sixty to ninety feet deep containing a mixture of anti-tank and anti-personnel mines were followed by anti-tank ditches and barriers, some twelve feet deep and up to nine feet wide, filled with dragon-tooth metal spikes, burned-out vehicles and concrete blocks, as well as fifty-five-gallon drums of napalm that could be detonated by remote control. Infantry brigades were dug into deep trenches, reinforced with concrete-coated steel mesh, wire or reeds—so well dug in, in fact, that they could not withdraw.[11]

Additionally, the Iraqi defenses were set up in layers. The first line was established three to ten miles from the Saudi border. Behind its minefields, barbed wire, ditches, berms, and oil-filled trenches stood small units (platoons and companies) of Iraqi soldiers. Ten miles or so from the first line was a second line of defense, identical to the first, except defended by larger military units. Brigades, each consisting of several thousand soldiers, defended the second line. The Iraqis hoped that any coalition forces that broke through the first line of defense would get caught in a killing zone between the two layers. Finally, behind the second layer of

defense were Iraq's operational reserves, organized in the largest military formations, divisions, and corps. Iraq's best troops, the Republican Guards represented the main reserve elements. Heavily armed with artillery and Iraq's best tanks, T-72s, the Republican Guard was responsible for mounting a fierce counterattack against coalition forces.

The Iraqis did not attempt to construct a defensive line along the several hundreds of miles of Saudi-Iraqi border west of

After the air war, the coalition turned to its ground forces to push the Iraqis out of Kuwait. These tank crewmen await battle in the Saudi Arabian desert.

Kuwait. The sheer length of the border made it impossible for the Iraqis to defend. Besides, they doubted that the coalition would attempt to move its forces to this far western region to bypass Kuwait and move directly into Iraq because it seemed too difficult to cross hundreds of miles of featureless desert in a region without roads or facilities to support a large-scale ground assault. The Iraqis were wrong. This was the main invasion route when coalition ground operations began in late February 1991.

Coalition Strategy

General Norman Schwarzkopf, the coalition's military commander, needed a strategy to overcome the natural advantages of the defenders. He found it in a military maneuver as old as military history itself—the flanking maneuver. According to his plan, the main thrust of coalition forces would come in several prongs from Saudi Arabia as much as three hundred miles to the west of the Saudi-Kuwaiti border. The objectives were Basra in southeastern Iraq and Highway 8, the main link between Baghdad and Basra. If the coalition could seize Highway 8 and take Basra, Iraqi forces would be cut in half. Iraqi troops in Kuwait would be completely cut off from supplies and reinforcements. Once cut off, those forces would be easily defeated. A far western prong of the offensive would sweep around Iraqi forces. An eastern prong would force the Iraqis to come out and fight, sacrificing all of the advantages of fighting from prepared defensive posi-

As military commander of the coalition, General Norman Schwarzkopf determined the strategy that would be employed for the ground war—the flanking maneuver.

tions. There was also a second thrust, a south-to-north movement directly into Kuwait, that was intended both to attack Iraqi forces and to divert them from the main attack to the west. At the same time, coalition efforts to divert Iraqi attention from the west were further bolstered by the threat to launch a large-scale amphibious landing by U.S. Marines on the coastline near Kuwait City.

Mounting an Amphibious Threat

The coalition placed an impressive flotilla of ships in the northern end of the Persian Gulf. Many of the naval vessels were amphibious assault ships or ships that would support a sea-based invasion. On board those ships were seventeen thousand U.S. Marines ready to spearhead any amphibious operation. Of all of the world's armed forces, none had more experience conducting amphibious assaults than the marines. They were well equipped and very well trained.

For putting men ashore, the marines had at their disposal 31 large amphibious assault ships; 17 hovercraft, called landing craft air cushion ships; and 115 smaller amphibian assault vehicles. These ships could land troops with equipment and small arms, tanks, antitank vehicles, and light armored vehicles. Small carriers put 19 Harrier jump-jets and 136 helicopters near the coast for air support and transport. Large naval vessels would offer fire support while aircraft carriers would provide an assortment of supporting aircraft. Additionally, the assault ships were supported by 13 landing craft utility ships, a repair ship, and 5 command vessels. Large maritime positioning ships that had brought equipment to the Gulf stood by to put supplies on land once the marines secured a beachhead.

Taken as a whole, the marine amphibious assault threat was substantial. The marines themselves were confident of success and pressed hard for authorization to go. Yet Iraq's coastal defenses were thick and dangerous. Fearing an amphibious assault by U.S. Marines, the Iraqis had devoted substantial effort to fortifying the Kuwaiti coast. They deployed a total of eleven divisions, each consisting of ten thousand to twenty thousand soldiers: seven divisions of light infantry and four heavier, armored divisions. Air defenses were set up to shoot down marine helicopters. Apartment complexes and other buildings along the coast were turned into armed fortresses. And, in order to make an amphibious operation as difficult and as bloody as possible, the Iraqis dug an elaborate system of berms, trenches, bunkers, minefields, and antitank ditches; buried tanks; and placed barbed wire to block exit routes from the beaches. To disable and destroy incoming ships, the Iraqis laid more than one thousand mines along the beaches and in shallow waters and placed barbed wire and obstacles underwater. If the marines attempted to come ashore in this area, the Iraqis intended to make them pay dearly.

Coalition commanders believed that five days of coastal bombing and bombardment and eighteen days of mine-clearing efforts were needed before an amphibious attack could be launched. Further, the damage to Kuwaiti properties near the coast would have been severe. For these reasons, Desert Storm commanders decided against an early amphibious operation. They wanted to keep the option open, however. If either the great sweep to the west of Iraqi forces or the direct south-to-north attack by Arab and U.S. Marine forces became bogged down, commanders were prepared to authorize an amphibious attack.

Loaded with vehicles, a landing craft speeds towards shore.

Though this large-scale landing never came, the marines and their amphibious assault vessels contributed substantially to the success of ground operations. The marines conducted several highly publicized, amphibious exercises in Oman and Saudi Arabia, and they carried out small-scale probing actions and false moves, or feints, keeping the Iraqis off balance and fearful of an amphibious landing. Without firing a shot, the marines kept as many as six Iraqi divisions tied down along the coast, away from the actual areas of combat.

Dealing with Minefields and Fortified Positions

Even though Iraqi forces were preoccupied along the coast, the actual attacking forces still had to cope with the Iraqis' thick defen-

sive positions. The first forces to move into Kuwait were the marines and the Arab troops. Warships provided important support for these forces. Two surface action groups organized around powerful U.S. battleships, the *Missouri* and the *Wisconsin,* provided gunfire support. These two World War II–era battleships, surpassed in size only by aircraft carriers, were used to pound Iraqi forces with huge shells. The main firepower of the *Missouri* and the *Wisconsin* came from their nine sixteen-inch guns. These huge guns fired shells that weighed almost as much as a small car and could reach targets twenty-five miles away. The two battleships

The World War II–era battleships USS Wisconsin *and USS* Missouri *fired shells at Iraqi installations during the ground war.*

pounded Iraqi installations and positions along the coast with over one thousand tons of shells. While this pounding was a boon to the marines and Arab troops, they still had to confront Iraqi defenses head on and they had to avoid getting trapped in kill boxes. Minefields were their first deadly obstacles.

Coalition forces were prepared for the challenge. First, they benefited from excellent intelligence about the location of minefields, gathered from reconnaissance planes and spy satellites, Iraqi troops who had surrendered, and hundreds of U.S. Marines and special forces who infiltrated behind enemy lines. In some cases, antimine specialists would carefully probe the ground, find mines, and make them explode from a safe distance. Additionally, the United States possessed specialized and sophisticated equipment for antimine operations.

The Iraqis had hoped that minefields would cause major casualties and expose coalition forces to fierce counterattacks after they became bogged down in the minefields. Instead, the coalition attackers rolled right over these first lines of defense. Large earthmovers flattened sand berms and barbed wire and pushed antitank barriers aside. Fire-fighting equipment for extinguishing ditches of burning oil was available but was usually unnecessary because in the days leading up to the ground offensive, coalition aircraft had used incendiary bombs to ignite most of the ditches. Additionally, due to the speed and power of the coalition advance, the stunned Iraqis simply could not manage to ignite the remaining

Disabling Mines

Antimine operations constituted another area in which wealth and high technology gave the coalition great military advantage. Most mines were disabled by specialized equipment. Planes dropped large concussion bombs designed to detonate and destroy mines. On the ground, one of the most effective means for dealing with mines was a device called a line-charge rocket launcher. A rocket launched three two-inch-wide steel cables one hundred feet down the minefield. Each cable carried more than a ton of plastic explosives divided into numerous small charges. The explosives were safely detonated by remote control, setting off almost all mines in the area of coverage. In a few instances, the Iraqis placed barbed wire or even chicken wire around the minefields, blocking and snarling the long line-charge steel cables, thus making the line charges ineffective. Most of the time, however, the line charges cleared away mines with great efficiency.

After the line-charge rockets were fired, specially equipped M-60 tanks moved in. Using special plows and rakes, the tanks brought the remaining mines to the surface, where they could be easily detonated or simply bypassed. The combination of line-charge rockets and antimine vehicles allowed coalition forces to move rapidly through minefields, clearing out and marking lanes through which attacking forces could pass. In some places, the mines were so dense that mine-clearing units were unable to open as many lanes as planned. Likewise, some mine-clearing and other armored vehicles were damaged or destroyed in the process. But overall, training, intelligence, and technology paid off. Despite the Iraqis' elaborate defensive preparations, minefields claimed but few casualties and failed to slow the rapid advance of coalition forces.

ditches. Artillery and air strikes destroyed bunkers. Heavy ramps allowed tanks to get over ditches and berms. Infantry fighting vehicles, armored personnel carriers, tanks, and other vehicles simply rolled over the Iraqi positions. Armored bulldozers drove along the edges of Iraqi trenches, collapsing them and crushing and burying Iraqi soldiers who had not fled or surrendered.

Iraqi Artillery and the Coalition's Antiartillery Weapons

As successful as they were in overrunning the first lines of defenses, coalition troops had to be concerned about Iraq's ability to stand up to the coalition's offensive. Even as they passed the first lines of defense, coalition troops were coming into range of Iraqi artillery. Iraq's large artillery pieces were numerous and modern and, in some cases, had longer-range striking power than coalition artillery. Iraq possessed roughly a dozen major types of artillery pieces, which fired shells ranging from four to eight inches wide. Coalition planners believed that Iraq had a total of about four thousand of the big guns. Not only might those guns inflict losses on coalition attackers, but they also threatened to stun the attackers, opening breaches in their formations that would allow the Iraqis to mount counteroffensives. Consequently, artillery pieces were high-priority targets for the coalition.

During the air campaign, Iraq was able to conceal many artillery pieces, and others escaped detection and destruction be-

cause of their mobility. Even so, coalition air attacks took a serious toll on Iraqi artillery, and the land war brought new attacks on those weapons. Only a small portion of Iraq's artillery pieces were self-propelled; the large majority were towed by trucks and other vehicles. Towed artillery pieces were easier to destroy because they could not be moved as rapidly as self-propelled ones, and the trucks that moved them were not armored. When under attack, the Iraqi artillery rounds were dangerously exposed and were likely to blow up, and Iraqi soldiers were more likely to desert the unprotected trucks than were the crews of self-propelled artillery pieces.

The attacks on Iraqi artillery were savage. A major weapon used by the coalition in its effort to suppress Iraqi artillery fire was its own artillery. Iraqi artillery may have had great range, but coalition artillery was devastatingly accurate. A combination of dominance on the battlefield and high technology accounted for the huge coalition advantage in accuracy. Iraqi forces, pinned down and deprived of battlefield intelligence, could not find and attack an enemy on the move. The coalition, on the other hand, was able to use sophisticated computers to feed artillery gunners with data about weather (wind, heat, and humidity) and target location. The target location and fire-control systems were excellent. Coalition gunners could find their targets and adjust their fire with the information they received from forward observers and aircraft.

They also had something called fire-finder radar, which rapidly tracked shells coming from Iraqi guns and fed the data into computers that calculated the trajectory of those shells and traced their origins. The data was instantly transmitted to coalition artillery, which immediately counterfired. Before the wildly fired Iraqi shells could ever hit a target, coalition counterfire destroyed the Iraqi guns that had fired them. In the same way that Iraqi antiaircraft gunners learned that they were practically committing suicide by turning on their radar, Iraqi artillerymen learned that firing their guns would bring steel rain on their heads in a matter of moments.

Steel rain was, in fact, the term used by the Iraqis for some of the American artillery fire. Some 155-millimeter and 8-inch artillery shells contained small bomblets instead of the normal single large explosive charge. The 155-millimeter shells spread 88 bomblets over the target area while the 8-inch shells dispersed 180 bomblets. At the first sign of this steel rain, Iraqi troops often abandoned their guns and ran for their lives.

Another fierce and highly effective source of steel rain was the American multiple-launch rocket system (MLRS). A single battery contains twelve launching

---

With technologically superior equipment, the coalition utilized its own artillery to suppress Iraqi artillery fire.

tubes that are fired almost simultaneously. Each rocket delivers 644 bomblets. Thus, the MLRS could saturate a target area with roughly 8,000 bomblets in a matter of moments. Because the tubes could be speedily reloaded, a single MLRS battery could lay down an immense wall of fire on its target. The whooshing and high-pitched screaming of the rockets as they fired only reinforced their image of great power. Often, after coming under fire from an MLRS barrage, Iraqi positions would collapse, with soldiers pouring out to surrender.

Iraqi Armor

Along with artillery, tanks were the other major source of punching power in Iraq's arsenal. Providing both mobility and firepower, Iraqi tanks also had the potential to inflict heavy casualties on coalition forces. Intelligence reports indicated that Iraq had four thousand to five thousand tanks, more than any country in the world except the United States and the Soviet Union. The number of Iraqi tanks was impressive, but their quality was a different story. The majority of tanks were fairly old Soviet models, mostly T-55s and T-62s. The Iraqis also fielded the newer Soviet T-72. (For Soviet tank models, the United States and its European allies used a *T*, signifying "tank," and a number, referring to the year the tank first appeared in service.)

The T-62 is a slightly improved version of the T-55. Neither tank is particularly combat effective by modern standards. Their fire-control systems are not very good,

and they cannot fire accurately while on the move. They require much maintenance and break down frequently. In addition, their armor is not strong. It is easily penetrated by the two main types of antitank rounds used by the United States and its allies. One uses extremely high velocity to penetrate armor; the other round, called high-explosive antitank (HEAT), employs a shaped charge, which is a warhead that directs the explosion forward, sending a molten stream of metal through the armor.

Coalition planners had to be more respectful of the several hundred T-72s fielded by the Iraqis. Using a laser rangefinder, some T-72s could efficiently find targets and lock onto them. At a range of slightly less than a mile, T-72s could be quite accurate. Some T-72s were also equipped with better armor, protecting them against many of the Coalition's antitank weapons. Still, even the best T-72s had important weaknesses. They were not very fast, and their accuracy at longer ranges was quite poor.

Even so, tanks are powerful fighting machines, especially when they are plentiful and are supported by other armored vehicles. Iraq also possessed approximately six thousand armored personnel carriers (APCs) and one thousand infantry fighting vehicles (IFVs). Armored personnel carriers are less heavily armed than tanks or IFVs. Their primary weapons are machine guns, which pose a threat to exposed troops, but not to other armored forces. The primary

A destroyed Iraqi T-72 lies abandoned in the Kuwaiti desert.

value of APCs is in their ability to increase mobility on the battlefield. About twenty Iraqi soldiers could move across the battlefield at approximately forty miles per hour in the armored safety of each of these Soviet-made wheeled vehicles. Iraq's Soviet-built IFVs, though much less powerful than tanks, were equipped with armor-piercing tracer rounds and high-explosive incendiary rounds, both designed to penetrate the armor of opposing forces lighter than tanks. They also carried machine guns and grenade launchers. Capable of rapid movement and able to cross water, IFVs were dangerous because they increased the power of Iraq's armored forces, enabling them to mount stiffer resistance and stronger counterattacks.

Coalition Tank-Killers: Airpower

On paper, Iraq's armored forces looked impressive. As it turned out, however, there were several thousand fewer Iraqi armored pieces in the Kuwaiti theater of operations than coalition planners had believed. Moreover, coalition forces had an assortment of weapons that were effective at fighting tanks.

Iraqi tank crews were constantly fearful of attacks from the air. After Iraq's air defenses were crippled and its air force defeated, coalition aircraft were free to hunt and kill tanks. The hunt-and-kill operations were greatly aided by the coalition's abundant intelligence and reconnaissance capabilities. Airpower was used with deadly effect against Iraq's armored forces. A-10 Thunderbolts and Apache helicopters were the most deadly of the airborne tank-killers.

Even those tanks buried in the sand were not safe. The coalition used F-111 bombers with sophisticated radar to find the buried tanks, and then they "painted" them with radar. Five-hundred-pound bombs which used sensors to lock onto the radar-painted tanks, were then used to destroy them. Other coalition attack aircraft with laser units joined in this mission, called "tank-plinking." Most Iraqi tanks were not buried in the ground, and were even easier to find and attack.

Coalition Tank-Killers: Missiles

For almost half a century, the United States had planned for war against the Soviet Union, which had by far the world's biggest fleet of tanks and other armored pieces. Since the United States and its European allies could not match the Soviets in armor, they had invested heavily in cheaper tank-killing weapons. Consequently, the United States had a large inventory of antitank missiles. Mavericks and Hellfires were two types. Another important one was the TOW (tube-launched, optically tracked, wire-guided) missile. The TOW (pronounced "toe") uses a wire connected to the sight for guidance.

As the missile flies forward, the thin wire rapidly unspools, and the missile is directed toward whatever target is in the gunner's sights. The TOW has two limitations. First, it cannot be used against unseen targets. Distance, obstacles, smoke, and dust all render the TOW useless. Second, in some instances, the TOW operator must keep his head dangerously exposed in order to keep the missile on target.

Nonetheless, the TOW is a simple but effective missile. It can be carried by many vehicles, some of which eliminate the problem of the vulnerable soldier's head. The TOW was especially important in the rapid movement of the coalition's main offensive in the west. Coalition forces racing to cut off Highway 8 had to be fairly light; tanks and other heavy equipment simply could not keep up. If coalition forces encountered Iraq's elite armored divisions before their own tanks arrived, they would need some means to fight them. Air support was one such means. Long-range helicopters armed with TOWs constituted another. Equipped with TOW antitank missiles, those helicopters were able to destroy Iraqi tanks.

Light, mobile vehicles armed with TOWs represented a third defense against Iraqi tanks. TOWs were mounted on high-mobility multipurpose wheeled vehicles (HMMWVs, pronounced "Humvees"), popularly known as "Hummers." Designed as a replacement for the jeep, the wide-bodied Hummer can zip along at sixty-five miles per hour carrying a load of twenty-five hundred pounds. With TOW missiles

aboard, the fifty-thousand-dollar vehicle could go toe-to-toe with the far costlier enemy tanks.

Two soldiers prepare to fire their TOW (tube-launched, optically tracked, wire-guided) missile.

The Coalition's IFVs and APCs

The coalition had IFVs and APCs just as Iraq had, and because the coalition fought a war of rapid mobility, it put them to better use. In addition to moving troops more efficiently than the Iraqis, the coalition was also able to bring much more firepower to bear with its armored vehicles. Iraq's Soviet-built IFVs were good, but the coalition's were outstanding. For the coalition, the premier IFV was the American M2 Bradley Fighting Vehicle. Bradleys were not designed as tank-killers, but their twenty-five-millimeter cannon were devastating against almost everything else. They even did serious damage to Iraqi tanks. The Bradleys' cannon used a thermal (heat-detecting) gunsight that made it lethal even in the midst of oil fires and sandstorms. The Bradleys also held up quite well on the battlefield. Because of their mobility and the coalition's ability to "blind" the Iraqis, only a few dozen of the sixteen hundred Bradleys in the Kuwaiti

theater of operations sustained damage. Of those, only three were put out of commission (one in a lethal instance of friendly fire).

The American M2 Bradley was the most effective IFV (infantry fighting vehicle) fielded by the coalition in the Persian Gulf War.

Coalition Tank-Killers: Tanks

The coalition also had armored vehicles that were highly effective as tank-killers—their own tanks. Though fewer in number, the coalition's tanks were certainly superior to the Iraqis'. Three stand out: the American M1A1 Abrams, the American M60A1, and the British Chieftain. When it was first produced, the Chieftain boasted the heaviest armor plating of any tank in the world.

At four hundred millimeters (almost thirty-two inches), this armor protected the Chieftain against all but direct hits from the most powerful armor-piercing shells. With a laser range-finder for targeting and the ability to move at almost fifty miles per hour, the Chieftain had great mobility and success as a tank-killer.

The American M60A1, though fairly old (the last M60s were produced in 1987), was still a good tank. The M60A1 was equipped with modern reactive armor, which was designed to produce something most civilians would think tank designers would least want—explosions! Reactive armor is actually lined with numerous small explosive charges. When hit by an enemy round, the charges in the area of impact detonate. This actually weakens the armor-penetrating effects of HEAT rounds, as the jet of extremely hot gases that would otherwise burn through the armor is spread out and deflected. With thermal sights, M60A1 gunners could find their targets by their heat, even when visibility was extremely poor due to dust and the smoke from oil fires.

The best coalition tank, and arguably the best tank in the world, was the American M1A1 Abrams. In its early stages of development, the Abrams had suffered delays, cost overruns, and equipment failure. Many had given up on the Abrams, considering it a wasteful and impractical project. But the mature M1A1 that was deployed in large numbers against Iraq was a superb weapon. Tanks are notorious for their maintenance problems, and in its developmental stages, the M1A1 broke down frequently. In the

A highly reliable and technologically advanced tank, the M1A1 Abrams caused considerable damage to Iraqi forces.

Persian Gulf, however, the Abrams was highly reliable despite the heat and sand that makes desert warfare so demanding.

The M1A1 had it all: speed and maneuverability, an advanced thermal system for locating targets by their heat signatures, an excellent computerized fire-control system that allowed it to fire accurately while on the move, and several types of highly effective armor-penetrating rounds. Additionally, the Abrams featured Chobham armor, a composite of steel plates, plastic or aluminum casings, and ceramic blocks in a waferlike design. Composite armor is very hard to penetrate.

With almost two thousand M1A1s, the United States had a devastating weapon against Iraqi tanks. Even Iraq's best tank, the T-72, was no match for the Abrams. In one instance, an M1A1 got stuck in mud and was left behind by its unit to wait for a recovery vehicle. In their book *From Shield to Storm*, James Dunnigan and Austin Bay describe what happened next:

Three T-72s appeared and attacked. The first fired from under 1,000 meters, scoring a hit with a shaped-charge (high explosive round) on the M1A1's frontal armor. The hit did no damage. The M1A1 fired a 120-mm armor-piercing round that penetrated the T-72 turret, causing an explosion that blew the turret into the air. The second T-72 fired another shaped-charge round, hit the frontal armor, and did no damage. The T-72 turned to run,

and took a 120-mm round in the engine compartment and blew the engine into the air. The last T-72 fired a solid shot (sabot) round from 400 meters. This left a groove in the M1A1's frontal armor and bounced off. The T-72 then backed up behind a sand berm and was completely concealed from view. The M1A1 depressed its gun and put a sabot round through the berm, into the T-72, causing an explosion.[12]

This encounter was fairly typical. Iraqi armor was simply outclassed and overwhelmed by the diverse and technologically advanced antiarmor capabilities of the United States and its partners. In fact, blinded and gravely wounded by the air campaign, Iraqi forces were completely outmatched.

Coalition Effectiveness in Combat

When the ground offensive began, the coalition put all of these weapons to use against Iraq's armored forces. With numerous effective command and control links, these weapons could be well directed and coordinated, even as coalition offensives moved across the battlefield at record speed. In a mere two days the Iraqis were almost completely defeated, and after four days all fighting ceased.

Separate coalition units moved northward toward a number of objectives. As they approached the Iraqis, they laid down withering salvos from their big guns. In one battle, U.S. Army units began an attack on a Republican Guard division with a barrage by artillery and multiple rocket launchers that was, according to author Rick Atkinson in his book *Crusade,* as devastating "as any ever unleashed in combat."[13] Numerous artillery tubes joined ten MLRS batteries in pounding an area only twelve by twenty-five miles. In the course of thirty minutes, more than eleven thousand artillery rounds and six hundred thousand MLRS bomblets rained down on that small area. When the barrage stopped and American troops surged forward, the Iraqis had little fight left in them.

As coalition troops pierced the Iraqis' defensive positions, they usually encountered brief fire from machine guns and small arms and inaccurate rounds from mortar and artillery. Some Iraqi tank crews intended to sit passively until coalition troops had passed and then they would fire on them. But as they realized just how deadly the fire was from Hellfire, Maverick, and TOW missiles and from M1A1 tanks, they usually decided to abandon their tanks, wisely concluding that those tanks were not weapons of offense but death-traps for their own crews.

In some places, Iraqi troops stood their ground and fought hard. Resistance seldom lasted long, however, and coalition casualties were remarkably low. Faced with firepower the likes of which they had never seen, most Iraqi soldiers were content to surrender. In some cases, the spectacle of

Iraqis looking to surrender was almost comical. In one instance, the driver of an American military truck, which was stuck in the mud and was awaiting assistance, was surprised to see an approaching Iraqi unit led by a tank. The entire unit surrendered to the American driver after the Iraqi tank

JSTARS

If armored forces were the musicians and instruments of Desert Storm, the command, control, and intelligence (C^3I) system was the conductor that made those weapons into a symphony of war. In this category, the situations of Iraq and the coalition could not have been more different. Iraq's C^3I system was shattered and most of its elements were destroyed or compromised. The coalition, in contrast, had numerous secure command and control links. One of those was a battle-management aircraft called the joint surveillance target attack radar system, or JSTARS (pronounced "jaystars").

The JSTARS is the land-warfare version of the AWACS. Like the AWACS, it utilizes a modified version of a Boeing 707 packed with computers and communications consoles and equipped with highly advanced radar systems. Making their first appearance in hostilities in Desert Storm, JSTARS aircraft did much to lift the fog of the battlefield for the coalition by detecting, identifying, and tracking Iraqi equipment. Like AWACS planes, they provided comprehensive and detailed aerial surveillance of each battle area. Regardless of weather, JSTARS aircraft could distinguish tanks from trucks and provide mapping data on battle-area terrain. This wealth of information was then forwarded to coalition ground and air forces, which then subjected the Iraqis to withering attacks. The JSTARS greatly enhanced the coalition's ability to target and destroy tanks and other weapons, and at the same time it helped avoid friendly-fire accidents.

obligingly pulled the American truck out of the mud.

The general pattern was the same in each of the sectors of attack. In the far west, the U.S. and French forces raced across the Iraqi desert unopposed. Aided by several reconnaissance techniques—including on-the-ground analysis conducted earlier by special forces—these forces moved confidently over ground solid enough to bear the weight of military vehicles. Using global positioning satellites and other sophisticated navigational aids, they easily crossed the featureless terrain directly toward their chosen destinations. And, aided by C-130s and helicopters that leapfrogged ahead with supplies (including huge "bladder" bags filled with fuel), large units of soldiers and equipment could surge forward without waiting for supplies to catch up. They moved rapidly to Highway 8 in Iraq, and from there, east to Basra.

Farther to the east, units of the U.S. VII Corps moved north, then turned sharply to the east to attack Iraqi forces. Even those Republican Guard units that had escaped serious damage during the six-week air campaign were unable to offer much resistance. With their formations and defensive lines facing south, they were not able to adjust fast enough to resist the heavy firepower and rapid movement of coalition troops.

In the east, along and near the coast, the two marine divisions and the Arab forces took surprisingly few casualties as they moved north. As they neared Kuwait City, their commanders worried about the potential costs of forcing the Iraqis out of the city. Both civilian and coalition casualties would probably be high. Contemporary military experience showed that in the rubble and building-to-building fighting of urban warfare, combat was especially bloody. Fortunately, the fears were groundless. With defeat looming, the Iraqis abandoned Kuwait City, though not before looting it of everything they could carry.

Most soldiers would never get to enjoy their loot, however. By seizing Highway 8

Coalition warplanes attacked thousands of military vehicles and stolen cars attempting to enter Iraq on what came to be known as "the Highway of Death."

and Basra, the coalition had cut off their retreat. Though some units succeeded in scampering back to Iraq, tens of thousands of Iraqi soldiers were trapped. As they raced north on the only available highway, they were sitting ducks for coalition warplanes, which came after them in angry swarms. Since one war objective was to degrade Iraq's military power so it could not soon threaten its neighbors, the coalition demanded that the Iraqis leave their heavy weapons behind. Instead, the JSTARS and other surveillance aircraft saw an immense traffic jam of thousands of military vehicles and stolen cars attempting to flee into Iraq.

Most did not get very far. The attacking jets first went after the head and rear of this massive convoy of retreat. The destroyed vehicles at both ends of the column made it very difficult for the rest to escape. It then became a turkey shoot for the airborne troops. Shortly afterward, photographs in the media showed thousands of burned out vehicles clustered closely together along what came to be called "the Highway of Death." On day four of the ground offensive, the war was over. Within days, all Iraqi forces were gone from Kuwait.

Airpower brought Iraqi forces to their knees, and the large weapons systems of land warfare delivered the final blow. But there were additional ingredients in the mix of coalition forces that produced such stunning success in what had truly become the age of information warfare.

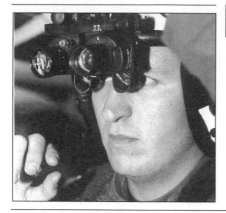

Chapter 6

Making Weapons Work

Iraq was overwhelmed by the array of powerful, advanced weapons (primarily American ones) brought to bear by the coalition. When the average person thinks of war, it is naturally tank battles, artillery duels, and aerial combat that come to mind, and without a doubt, these major weapons systems were vitally important in the Persian Gulf War. But there were other, less visible kinds of weapons behind those conventional ones: information dominance, superior training, well-equipped special forces, and support from industry, not to mention the financial resources that made all of these important components of military success possible.

Information

Students of politics often say that information is power. The same applies to military affairs. In warfare, the absence of information is absolutely deadly. Military analysts often use the term *fog of war,* which was coined by the Prussian military theorist Carl von Clausewitz and refers to the confusion that arises when large numbers of rapidly moving soldiers are engaged in combat, often over a large expanse of territory. Throughout history, veterans of battles have described the utter chaos that takes hold of the battlefield, as soldiers find it hard to tell friend from foe or to know who is winning or losing. War also creates conditions that are literally like fog, when smoke and dust on the battlefield make it physically impossible to see.

In the war for Kuwait, only the Iraqis were seriously hampered by this fog. Coalition commanders, officers, and individual soldiers, on the other hand, benefited from an unprecedented amount of information. The coalition was able to use its superior wealth, power, and technology both to increase the amount of information available to itself and to blind the Iraqi opponent.

Because Iraqi forces fought primarily from fixed defensive positions, they did not have the same intense need for information that coalition forces had. Even so, lack of information was a severe handicap. Without good battlefield intelligence, the Iraqis could not adjust their artillery fire to hit moving troops. When small Iraqi units attempted to venture out at night to conduct raids or reconnaissance missions, they had to do so without the sophisticated navigational aids readily available to coalition troops. As a result, they often became disoriented in the dark, sometimes getting hung up in their own minefields.

In contrast, coalition troops possessed vast amounts of military information that would have been unimaginable to earlier generations of warriors. Unlike Iraqi troops, coalition forces had sophisticated computers, sensors, dense communications systems, satellites and spy planes, joint surveillance and target attack radar system (JSTARS) and AWACS aircraft, global positioning system sets, radar, night vision equipment, and more. These technologies brought huge advantages in command, control, communications, and intelligence (C³I). Like logistics, superiority in C³I is less noticeable than in weaponry, but it is absolutely vital to military success.

Eyes in the Sky

Satellites and spy planes provided a wealth of intelligence. Five American KH-11 (Keyhole) satellites equipped with telescopes provided reams of high-resolution photographs of sites in Iraq and Kuwait. The photographs were transferred by relay satellite to a facility in Maryland, which then transmitted them by satellite to U.S. forces in Saudi Arabia. Some Keyholes were equipped with infrared sensors capable of taking pictures at night. Some were equipped with electronic listening devices to intercept Iraqi communications. Mentor and Vortex signals intelligence satellites also enabled the coalition to eavesdrop on Iraqi communications. A Lacrosse radar satellite provided images even when cloud cover was heavy. Several planes performed similar missions. The RF-4, a converted version of the older F-4 Phantom fighter, provided photos of Iraqi forces and targets, as did the old U-2 spy plane and its modernized version, the TR-1.

Intelligence provided by satellites and spy planes was enormously useful to the coalition. The five-month interval between Iraq's invasion of Kuwait and the beginning of Desert Storm allowed the Defense Mapping Agency to accumulate thousands of photographs that were used to create the contour maps needed by the cruise missiles. Without the maps, there could have been no pinpoint strikes on downtown Baghdad targets on the first night of the air war. Photos from the sky also gave the United States and its allies a remarkably good picture of the military and industrial sites that would constitute the targets for the coalition bombing campaign.

Computers and Battlefield Intelligence

Coalition computers were far more numerous and advanced and coalition military

operations were computerized to a much greater extent than for the Iraqis'. Computers were everywhere, and they were indispensable to the military success of the coalition. Satellite systems could not have operated without dense networks of computers supporting them. Advanced weapons systems are loaded with computers; individual tanks and planes, for instance, rely on dozens, even hundreds, of computers. Only with the aid of large banks of computers were AWACS and JSTARS aircraft able to gather detailed information about vehicles and planes spread out over large patches of sky and ground and then provide that in-

The sophisticated technology at the coalition's disposal provided it with significant advantages over Iraq.

formation to coalition forces. Computers were also essential to the mammoth logistical operation that put troops, weapons, and supplies into the Persian Gulf. Computers kept track of inventories and suppliers, matched supplies to commanders' needs in the Gulf, and planned and coordinated transport operations.

If the coalition dominated the contest for large-scale information, its domination of small-scale or tactical intelligence was equally overwhelming. Wild Weasels and other radar-locating planes made it extremely dangerous for the Iraqis to turn on their radar, and coalition artillery with fire-finder radar had the same effect on Iraqi artillery. On the ground and in the air, radar, optical sensors, and heat-seekers allowed coalition forces to find and destroy Iraqi forces with devastating accuracy. If fighters with laser-guided bombs could not operate in cloudy conditions, those with infrared targeting systems could. Similarly, the advanced avionics of the fighters themselves allowed planes to navigate at night and during bad weather.

Iraqi soldiers might stumble and become disoriented in the dark. With night-vision goggles, however, the coalition's helicopter pilots and soldiers on the ground could operate almost as well in the dark as in daylight. The Iraqis assumed that a large-scale flanking operation across featureless desert would be impossible to navigate. They failed to reckon with the global positioning system units which allowed coalition divisions and individual soldiers alike to know their exact location twenty-four hours a day. The effectiveness of weapons was increased greatly by these information technologies.

Communications

Iraq's communications systems were in shambles. By contrast, the coalition had the most efficient communications system ever seen in combat.

The coalition had an immense need for secure communications. It is hard to appreciate just how large this need was. Millions of separate communications had to cross oceans daily. A single logistics line had to handle two-hundred thousand supply transactions every day. A worldwide communications and battle-management system performed limitless tasks. According to a September 1991 article in the *IEEE Spectrum* journal, a publication of the Institute of Electrical and Electronics Engineers,

> The system gave instructions to auto-targeting missile pods on fighter bombers and unmanned remotely piloted reconnaissance vehicles alike. These and other units, in turn, fed data back into the information-rich environment that planned missions, assembled target coordinates, searched digital libraries for data on terrain, directed more sensors or weapons to an area, ordered spare and replacement parts, and so on—usually under intense pressure of time.[14]

Much of this system had to be created from scratch. As with so many other aspects of Desert Storm, two things helped make this possible: wealth and technological sophistication. At the heart of the communications network were three satellites from the defense satellite communications system. Two were already in place. A third had to be programmed to change its stationary orbit from a position over the Pacific

Ocean to one over the Indian Ocean. More than one hundred large satellite dishes and numerous portable ones were set up in Saudi Arabia, and hundreds of desktop computers were shipped to Saudi Arabia and to military establishments in the United States and other coalition countries. Almost overnight, a vast and secure communications system was established, aiding all aspects of the Coalition's military

Helicopter pilots and soldiers could operate in the dark with night-vision goggles, giving them a significant advantage over Iraqi troops.

operations. Even without the damage from bombing, a country like Iraq could only dream of such a large and sophisticated system of military communications.

Special Forces

Not all the valuable military intelligence was collected by advanced technologies. Some was collected the old-fashioned way—by human reconnaissance and spying. Numbering close to ten thousand, special forces operating behind enemy lines performed valuable tasks. They conducted search and rescue operations for coalition soldiers and airmen stranded in Iraqi-held territory. They also added to the coalition's knowledge about Iraq's military capabilities. For example, special forces infiltrated Iraqi air-defense installations, in some cases taking components back to Saudi Arabia for analysis. In other cases, special forces helped find Iraqi military equipment so that it could be targeted by bombers. Eyes on the ground were valuable in finding small or concealed weapons. After finding military equipment, these personnel left behind electronic devices that would later be used to guide coalition bombers to the targets. Special forces were active in the hunt for Iraq's mobile Scud launchers. On the coast, navy SEALS helped deceive the Iraqis into believing that an amphibious assault was imminent, forcing the Iraqis to employ several whole divisions to defend against an invasion that never came.

Certainly one of the most important missions for special forces was in the preparation for the large, sweeping "Hail Mary" offensive in the west. The success of the offensive depended on surprise. Living for days at a time in tiny holes in the ground, small special-force units watched intently for Iraqi military movements or other signs that coalition military plans were compromised. Special forces also performed a crucial mission in investigating the desert terrain for the western offensive by scouting and taking soil samples in order to ensure that trucks and other vehicles would not get bogged down in the soft sands of the roadless desert.

The use of men to gather intelligence may have been old-fashioned, but the equipment they carried was not. Special-force soldiers carried radios, satellite communications gear, night-vision goggles, laser range-finders, periscopes, silencer-equipped weapons, and mines along with their food, ammunition, and digging gear. Taken as a whole, special forces represented an invaluable precision instrument in the coalition war machine, the "brains behind the brawn in Desert Storm,"[15] in the words of a former Green Beret.

Training

Weapons, even high-tech ones, are of little value without soldiers who are well trained in their use. Coalition soldiers—and American troops in particular—were very well trained. On the other hand, Iraqi forces "were uniformly poorly trained," according to Daryl G. Press in the fall 1997 issue of *International Security*. Thus, as Press concludes,

A Perilous Job

Life could be very difficult for the special forces. Dropped into Iraq by helicopters in the dead of night, some of these commandos found themselves dangerously close to Iraqi villages. For days at a time, they had to spend daylight hours hiding quietly in small holes in the hot desert with minimal water and supplies. In more than one instance, the small units were discovered by Iraqi civilians. The American commandos then had to make instant decisions about whether to kill the civilians (including a young girl and an old man) who stumbled upon them. It was a terrible predicament for the Americans. In each case, the commandos let moral considerations guide their decisions, and they allowed their discoverers to run away. But as the American commandos expected, those civilians immediately notified local authorities, who then called for troops.

Once, while deep inside Iraq, the American commandos watched in fear as a bus filled with Iraqi soldiers arrived. Outnumbered twenty to one, the Americans fought desperately while waiting to be rescued. The Americans were on the verge of being overwhelmed when an F-16 screamed overhead, dropping cluster bombs on the Iraqis. Evading ground fire, a rescue helicopter quickly followed. At great peril to pilot and crew, the approaching helicopter had to make sudden and sharp loops over and under power lines. Crew members were thrown violently about the helicopter, which barely avoided crashing. Arriving just in time, the rescue chopper immediately came under intense fire. Even as the commandos scrambled aboard the craft, a hail of bullets hit the propellers and shattered the windshield. The helicopter only barely managed to complete the rescue and get off the ground. Flying out of Iraq, the crew had to be intently alert for attacks by antiaircraft guns and missiles. But the mission succeeded, thanks to the soldiers who were willing to take mortal risks to save their comrades from certain death.

"The skill advantages of coalition troops were so large that skill alone would have led to one-sided battlefield outcomes, even had technology been even."[16]

Two huge American facilities were especially important: the army's National Training Center in Fort Irwin, California, and the air force's Fighter Weapons School at Nellis Air Force Base in Nevada. At both facilities, American soldiers receive live-fire training and conduct large force-on-force combat exercises. Live-fire training (in which soldiers shoot but are not shot at) gives soldiers the best understanding of how weapons actually perform. In their exercises, American tank crews fire real rounds and destroy trucks and armored vehicles, and pilots destroy remotely piloted aircraft with real air-to-air missiles. In force-on-force exercises, Americans fire computer-aided laser beams from their weapons instead of live fire.

Soldiers and air crews who fought in Desert Storm had already logged many hours in mock combat, as red teams pretending to be Soviet forces fought blue

In addition to superior technology, U.S. soldiers had an advantage over Iraqi troops in their high level of training.

American teams. The red teams employed Soviet combat doctrines and imitated Soviet tactics. In some cases, they were equipped with Soviet weapons. Since Iraq had received most of its weapons and combat training from the USSR, this training was extremely valuable.

At Nellis, planes were equipped with expensive instrument pods that transmitted all flight and combat data back to ground-based observers, who could analyze and evaluate the simulated combat in great detail. Air crews were then told exactly what they had done right and wrong. Similarly, the army's National Training Center could boast a complex $100-million network that monitored all aspects of simulated combat. Soldiers at the center also used combat simulators that had the look and feel of a real tank, fighter, or other combat vehicle. Inside the $250,000 simulators, the soldiers saw a realistic-looking battlefield on a computer screen and engaged in virtual combat against other soldiers on a military computer network.

Throughout the 1980s, U.S. Central Command (CENTCOM) conducted training exercises, large and small, to prepare for combat conditions in the Persian Gulf. Some exercises were conducted in the Mojave and other deserts in the western United States, and others took place in Egypt and elsewhere in the Middle East. As a result, CENTCOM was prepared for the heat, sandstorms, soft sands, and other conditions unique to the Persian Gulf region.

When the war with Iraq started, the air force created structures resembling communications towers, tank convoys, Scud launchers, and the concrete-reinforced revetments that the Iraqis used to protect their planes on the ground. In addition to seeing satellite photos of such targets, the pilots could practice finding and bombing them while actually flying at combat speed at altitudes of fifteen thousand feet and higher. Additionally, the training missions involved large numbers of aircraft flying in the same formations that were later used with devastating effect against the Iraqis.

Because of the costs of fuel, ammunition, targets, weapons maintenance, and training equipment, such rigorous training is enormously expensive. For countries like Iraq this kind of extensive and intensive training was not remotely affordable. The United States, on the other hand, had actually increased its training budgets by billions of dollars during the defense buildup of the 1980s.

The results of such costly and expensive training were dramatic. In air-to-air combat, highly trained American pilots easily defeated their Iraqi rivals, even when they flew comparable aircraft. Many pilots and other soldiers who fought in the Gulf reported a common experience: There were few surprises. Whatever they encountered in combat, they had already experienced in training and exercises. Having rehearsed the situations many times, they were usually ready for them. In fact, some of the training exercises had been even more demanding

Alone and Friendless: The Iraqi Predicament

Although the producers of coalition weapons aided the war effort, the same could not be said in Iraq. The Soviet Union and France were Iraq's major weapons suppliers, and they were not at all supportive.

The Soviet Union and Iraq had long been friends, and most of Iraq's weapons came from the USSR. Soviet leader Mikhail Gorbachev firmly opposed Iraq's act of aggression against Kuwait, however. Additionally, he needed American understanding and support for his own policies, so he did not want to antagonize Washington. Consequently, he refused to give Iraq any form of assistance. And, since all major Soviet industries, including defense, were owned by the government, this meant that Iraq would not receive any weapons, technical advice, intelligence, or assistance of any kind from the Soviets.

The Soviets also refused to provide spare parts for the Soviet-made weapons that filled most of Iraq's inventory. This was especially painful for Iraq since its military forces (like the Soviet forces on which they were modeled) had never invested much money in keeping stocks of spare parts. With few spare parts on hand, the Soviets refusing to provide any more, and coalition warplanes busily destroying both weapons and supplies, Iraq had desperate problems keeping its military equipment operational. Minor mechanical difficulties could doom military vehicles. Since they could not be repaired, they could only be cannibalized for parts to keep other vehicles in operation.

Moscow also ordered the withdrawal of Soviet military advisers from Iraq. In a move that would have been unthinkable throughout the cold war, the Soviets abandoned an important client state, leaving Iraq to face American might on its own. It was a move of great military importance to the United States.

After the Soviet Union, France was the second major supplier of Iraqi weapons. Although most French industries were privately owned or had mixed private-governmental ownership, the gov-ernment played a key role. The French government directed French firms to respect the international embargo against Iraq by not selling it any military goods. Worse still for Iraq, the French firms that refused to do business with Iraq reportedly provided important information to the United States. Some of Iraq's major weapons systems were made by the French—an antitank missile, a surface-to-air missile, combat helicopters, the Exocet, and the F-1 fighter. The United States and its coalition partners gained a deeper understanding of the strengths and weaknesses of such weapons through contacts with the French government and defense firms. Similarly, coalition commanders who engineered the bombing campaign reportedly gained knowledge about the design and layout of targets in Iraq (such as government buildings) from the European firms that had designed and built them.

The coalition learned about the French-made weapons it would confront in the Persian Gulf, such as this Mirage F-1 aircraft, when France joined the embargo against Iraq and disclosed helpful information to the coalition.

than combat. As one colonel told a journalist, "Almost every commander I talked to said the combat situations they found in Iraq were not as hard as what they'd encountered at NTC [the National Training Center]."[17] Like information technology, training significantly increased the effectiveness of coalition weapons, and it saved the lives of many soldiers.

Military equipment in need of repair, such as this fighter having its engine replaced, could be made operational again quickly due to the abundance of spare parts.

Support from Industry

The United States and its allies had yet another advantage over Iraq, a good relationship with the companies that made the weapons used in the Persian Gulf War. Spare parts were fairly easy to come by, and so was technical support. Not only was the United States able to work with the makers of American weapons, it was also able to learn a good deal about the strengths and weaknesses of some of Iraq's major weapons systems from the companies that produced them. Iraq's situation was just the opposite.

Unlike Iraq, the United States had thousands of engineers, technicians, and maintenance specialists available to keep weapons systems operational. These experts came from both the military and defense industries. Many were dispatched directly to the Persian Gulf. Others stayed in the United States but were constantly available to give advice and support through teleconferencing.

It is very demanding to keep high-tech weapons operational. Critics had warned that key weapons such as the M1A1 tank, the Bradley Fighting Vehicle, and the F-111 bomber, which had been plagued by problems in the development phase, would not be reliable in combat. With thousands of electronic components, modern weapons can break down easily, especially in the hot, dusty conditions of desert warfare.

Support made a world of difference. The American military was able to use computerized inventory systems to keep track of the millions of items and spare parts needed to keep military operations running smoothly. Close cooperation between the Pentagon and industry ensured that parts and items were readily available. And, an army of engineers, technicians, and maintenance specialists from the Department of Defense and from private industry kept

Collaboration Between Industry and the Military

Modern weapons can be used with maximum effect when there is a system in place to provide technical support and advice. The United States could afford a huge system of technical support; Iraq could not. One tactical fighter squadron of forty-eight F-15Es provides a good example. In addition to the 120 pilots and weapons-system operators, the F-15s were supported by more than eight-hundred military mechanics and technicians from industries that produced the fighter and its major components. As often happens in war, the Air Force discovered a particular mission for which the F-15E had not been designed. Early in the conflict, air force officials wanted to attack an airfield with cluster bombs. Fearing an encounter with defending Iraqi fighters, the commanders also wanted the F-15E to carry its usual supply of Sparrow air-to-air missiles. But they did not know if the F-15E would be aerodynamically sound carrying cluster bombs on one side and Sparrows on the other.

One solution would have been to improvise. The air force could simply have loaded the F-15Es with both bombs and Sparrows and then sent them off to attempt their missions. Instead, the problem was tackled by several teams from the air force and industry operating hundreds and even thousands of miles apart. Air force bases in Virginia and Ohio went to work on the problem along with the F-15E's producer, the McDonnell Douglas Corporation in St. Louis, Missouri. The three groups conducted wind-tunnel tests, flight tests, and other problem-solving approaches. Through teleconferencing, they were able to share their knowledge and the results of their test. After several conference calls and separate tests at the three facilities, the answer was relayed to the Persian Gulf: The plane could do it. Within hours, the Iraqi airfield was under attack by F-15Es carrying Sparrows and dropping cluster bombs.

tanks, fighters, and other military equipment operating. As a result, even the most advanced and complex systems were operational and mission-capable 90 percent of the time, an unprecedentedly high rate in wartime. Such success rates did not come cheaply. For the United States, spare parts, maintenance, and contractor support cost $20 billion, the single largest expense and one-third the total cost of the war. The United States spent an amount for combat support that was twice as much as Iraq's entire defense budget, demonstrating yet again the importance of wealth in the equation of combat effectiveness.

The Lessons of Desert Storm

As a military operation, Desert Storm was a resounding success for the United States and its coalition partners. Six weeks of bombing and a mere four-day ground campaign achieved a complete victory over Iraqi forces to liberate Kuwait. Not only were the Iraqis completely driven from Kuwait, but Iraq's military machine was severely damaged. Iraq's ability to threaten the peace and security of the Persian Gulf region was substantially reduced. Moreover, these goals were achieved without massive civilian or military casualties.

War Aims: Some Achieved, Some Not

The Coalition's primary war aims were achieved: Iraqi forces were expelled from Kuwait, and the Iraqi threat to other Persian Gulf nations was reduced. But the weapons that fulfilled the primary war aims so successfully were not as well suited to realize the secondary aims: removing Saddam Hussein from power and weakening Iraq's weapons-of-mass-destruction (WMD) programs. Coalition weapons imposed a humiliating defeat on Iraqi forces, but this was not enough to trigger Hussein's overthrow or death. Even highly accurate bombs were too blunt an instrument to serve as a tool of assassination.

Similarly, bombing did destroy many facilities associated with Iraq's numerous WMD programs, but many others were unknown to the coalition and thus escaped attack. This was especially true of chemical and biological weapons programs because much research and development could be done in very small facilities, which could not be identified as weapons labs. Bombing was entirely useless against the scientists whose knowledge could enable Iraq to develop these dreadfully deadly weapons.

If George Bush had been determined to achieve these secondary goals, he would have had to authorize a full-scale invasion of Iraq. In fact, many people criticized Bush

for ending the ground war after only four days. According to these critics, after reaching Basra, coalition forces should have gone on, all the way to Baghdad.

Despite the tremendous military advantages created by coalition weapons, President Bush believed the costs and risks of an invasion of Iraq were too great. A land war in Iraq would have involved Iraq's best forces fighting to defend the Iraqi homeland, and it might also have required difficult street-by-street fighting in Baghdad and other cities. Coalition casualties could have been very high. And, the real-

These Iraqi women stand in the ruins of a telecommunications center bombed during the six-week coalition air strike.

ization of coalition goals would have required a large and long occupation. Additionally, there were important political considerations. Many coalition members strongly opposed a large-scale invasion of Iraq, which would have been unpopular in the Persian Gulf region and thus damaging to U.S. political interests. Advanced, high-tech weapons could not alter these military and political realities.

Desert Storm: A Model for Future Conflicts Involving the United States?

Desert Storm raised big questions for the world and for the United States. Did it represent a revolution in warfare? Did it signify that the United States and its friends would have a ready ability to use high-tech weapons at low cost to accomplish foreign-policy goals? In particular, could the United States use force to shape the outcomes of the many ethnic conflicts that brought suffering and death to millions in Africa, the Balkans, and elsewhere?

In one sense, Desert Storm clearly did represent a military revolution. The combination of firepower and high technology enabled the U.S.-led coalition to achieve a major military objective against a well-armed adversary with remarkably few casualties to itself. Unfortunately, for the United States, however, the conditions that produced success in the Persian Gulf will not always be present in future conflicts.

Iraq committed a clear-cut act of aggression against a state with no other enemies. It was easy for the United States to isolate Iraq politically, and once isolated, Iraq had no one to turn to for economic or military assistance. The country could not

A man sifts through the remains of Iraqi armor destroyed during the conflict.

get weapons or supplies through trade. If it had had outside suppliers and foreign sanctuaries for its troops (as America's opponents did during the Korean and Vietnam Wars), it could have put up a stiffer fight. Another enemy might not be so isolated.

U.S. armed forces were equipped and trained to fight a foe like Iraq. Iraq's heavy army was acutely vulnerable to the unprecedented level of firepower the United States could bring to bear, especially in open desert terrain. U.S. forces were far less suited to combat in more difficult terrain such as mountains or jungles. In important respects, Desert Storm was warfare at its simplest. The bad guys wore Iraqi military uniforms, and soldiers were generally distinct and apart from civilians.

But few conflicts involve an army from one country invading and occupying another. Most contemporary wars are fought between people of different tribes, ethnic groups, or religions. As rival populations are mixed together, distinctions between friend and foe and combatants and noncombatants are often hard to make. Small mortar tubes, clubs, pistols, and machetes are the main weapons used by the ragtag armies, militias, and armed civilians that do most of the fighting. Ferocious firepower and impressive high-tech weapons are not effective against irregular forces, called guerrillas. Small units of lightly equipped fighters who employ hit-and-run tactics are difficult for modern armies to subdue, especially when they operate in

jungles and mountainous regions. In these conflicts, stealth fighters, cruise and Patriot missiles, AWACS planes, and Apaches are almost useless. Thus, in the years following Desert Storm, the United States and likeminded nations have experienced difficulties and frustrations in dealing with the immense human suffering brought about by civil wars in Bosnia, Somalia, Rwanda, Congo, Sierra Leone, and elsewhere.

The Weapons of Desert Storm and the Future of Interstate Warfare

The weapons that expelled Iraq from Kuwait revealed a revolution in conventional warfare involving large-scale military forces of two or more countries. If Desert Storm did not mean much to the warlords of Somalia, its implications were very clear to the governments and militaries of countries such as Russia, China, Iran, India, and North Korea. Any country considering itself a medium or great power must confront the lessons of the U.S.-led victory in the Persian Gulf.

Airpower truly came into its own in Desert Storm. The Gulf War showed that cruise missiles and advanced fighters armed with highly accurate missiles and bombs, and assisted by a fleet of support planes, can cause severe damage to an enemy's military forces and industries. The more economically developed a country, the more vulnerable its economy is to the ravages of airpower. Relatively cheap air defenses will not suffice to ward off lethal attacks from the air.

F-16 Falcons, carrying two-thousand-pound bombs, race toward Iraq. The Gulf War proved how effective air attacks can be in combat.

Similarly, ground warfare can be devastatingly effective. Success on the ground has always centered on mobility and firepower, facilitated by effective command and control. Mobility, in fact, multiplies the effects of firepower, so the combination of the two has always been highly prized but hard to achieve. Today, however, with the support of sensors, computers, satellites, airborne command and control, and a large logistical tail, armored forces—working in tandem with airpower—can achieve astonishing mobility on the battlefield, and they can pound an enemy with awesome firepower.

Desert Storm demonstrated that both the quality and the quantity of weapons make a big difference. Even against a modest-size country such as Iraq, the United States required hundreds of attack and support aircraft flying tens of thousands of sorties. Coalition forces consumed vast quantities of ordnance, drawing some stocks of precision-guided weaponry dangerously low. Big battalions still count for a great deal in military affairs. But more than ever before, the quality of weaponry was critical. Iraqi forces were devastated by cruise missiles and other smart weaponry and by the best fighters and tanks in the world. In turn, a dazzling array of sensors, computers, optics, and advanced materials embedded in and supporting those weapons showed just how important high technology is to military prowess.

Finally, Desert Storm shows that military superiority will require not only large arsenals of high-tech weapons, but also extensive training and an elaborate support structure. As is the case with most wars, Desert Storm also shows the importance of combined arms operations—land, air, and sea forces operating together—fighting under the guidance of well-conceived military doctrine.

Nothing is permanent in military affairs, and this includes the substantial advantages the United States brought to Desert Storm. The very decisiveness of the coalition victory over its fairly well-equipped Iraqi adversary created incentives for other potential enemies of the United States to look for ways to offset American power and

Arms Inspections in Iraq after Desert Storm

Although the coalition could not eliminate Iraq's programs for developing weapons of mass destruction(WMD), its overwhelming victory in Desert Storm did create a set of conditions favorable to disarmament. As part of the post–Desert Storm settlement, Iraq was forced to cooperate with international inspectors from the UN Special Commission (UNSCOM), which was created to rid Iraq of its WMD. As a result of UNSCOM inspections, the world was shocked to learn the size and scope of Iraq's nuclear, chemical, and biological weapons programs. Under UNSCOM supervision, large stocks of weapons, equipment, and materials were confiscated or destroyed.

For several years UNSCOM carried out inspections and used monitoring equipment to ensure that Iraq was not developing nuclear, chemical, or biological weapons. But it was a constant struggle. On countless occasions, the Iraqis blocked inspections and tried to conceal their efforts to develop WMD. Despite Iraq's lack of cooperation, several members of the UN Security Council opposed punitive actions. In 1998 the Iraqi government forced UNSCOM to leave the country. The Security Council demanded that Iraq cooperate with UNSCOM. The United States and Britain responded with a short but intense round of punitive bombing.

But many countries had simply grown tired of the struggle. Russia, China, and France favored lifting economic sanctions against Iraq in spite of Iraqi defiance. Meanwhile, the United States and Britain wanted to increase the pressure on Iraq. The Security Council searched for a compromise. Since Iraq refused to cooperate with an inspection led by the Australian head of UNSCOM, Richard Butler, the council sought to create a new inspection team under different leadership. At about the same time, reports surfaced of Iraqi efforts to fashion a weapon out of the bacteria that causes bubonic plague.

Iraq's determination to acquire WMD may well prove greater than the international community's will to stop it. Despite the coalition's victory in 1991, Iraq may yet succeed in developing some of these dreadful weapons. But at least U.S. actions during and after Desert Storm seriously retarded and complicated Iraq's schemes.

technological superiority. When the United States and its North Atlantic Treaty Organization allies bombed Serbia because of Serbian mistreatment of the population of Kosovo, the Serbs did a better job than the Iraqis at faking bomb targets and damage and at concealing real targets.

Technological monopolies seldom last long. In the years since the Gulf War, for example, global positioning system receivers and commercially produced high-resolution satellite photos have become more widely available. Inexpensive missiles will pose a growing threat to the large weapons platforms of land, sea, and air. Ballistic missile technologies continue to proliferate. Thus, future enemies of the United States may one day threaten American forces with missiles that are much more capable than Scuds. Even worse, the same applies to weapons of mass destruction. Asked about the lessons of Desert Storm, a general from India responded by saying that smaller countries should not consider waging war with the United States without nuclear weapons. Ironically, then, a war waged in part to strip Iraq of its weapons of mass destruction could result in other countries working that much harder to develop such dreadful weapons.

Nonetheless, for the rogue states of the world, the principal lesson of Desert Storm is that large-scale conventional conflict with the United States is extremely dangerous. Only a few countries have the wealth and technological sophistication to bring together all of the ingredients successfully employed by the United States and its partners in 1991. For the foreseeable future, only the United States will be capable of carrying out operations of the scale and intensity of Desert Storm.

☆ Notes ☆

Introduction: Desert Storm: The Inauguration of High-Tech War

1. Michael Sterner, "Closing the Gate: The Persian Gulf War Revisited," *Current History*, January 1997, p. 13.
2. Quoted in Peter Paret, ed., *Makers of Modern Strategy from Machiavelli to the Nuclear Age*. Princeton, NJ: Princeton University Press, 1986, p. 197.

Chapter 1: Projecting Power and Preparing for War

3. Quoted in Stanley Hoffmann, "Bush Abroad," *New York Review of Books*, November 5, 1990, p. 56.
4. Quoted in Lawrence Freedman and Efraim Karsh, *The Gulf Conflict, 1990–1991: Diplomacy and War in the New World Order*. Princeton, NJ: Princeton University Press, 1993, p. 362.
5. James A. Baker III with Thomas M. DeFrank, *The Politics of Diplomacy: Revolution, War, and Peace, 1989–1992*. New York: Putnam's, 1995, pp. 303–304.

Chapter 2: The Weapons of Air Domination

6. Michael R. Gordon and Bernard Trainor, *The Generals' War: The Inside Story of the Conflict in the Gulf*. Boston: Little,

Brown, 1995, p. 108.

Chapter 3: The Instruments of Airpower

7. Quoted in Rick Atkinson, *Crusade: The Untold Story of the Persian Gulf War*. New York: Houghton Mifflin, 1993, p. 217.

Chapter 4: Checking Iraqi Threats on Land and at Sea

8. Gordon and Trainor, *The Generals' War*, p. 230.
9. Quoted in Atkinson, *Crusade*, p. 237.
10. Norman Friedman, *Desert Victory: The War for Kuwait*. Annapolis, MD: Naval Institute Press, 1991, p. 204.

Chapter 5: The War on the Ground

11. Freedman and Karsh, *The Gulf Conflict, 1990–1991*, p. 362.
12. James F. Dunnigan and Austin Bay, *From Shield to Storm: High-Tech Weapons, Military Strategy, and Coalition Warfare in the Persian Gulf*. New York: William Morrow, 1992, pp. 294–95.
13. Atkinson, *Crusade*, p. 394.

Chapter 6: Making Weapons Work

14. *IEEE Spectrum*, "Warfare in the Information Age," September 1991, pp. 27–28.

15. Douglas Waller, "Secret Warriors," *Newsweek*, June 17, 1991, p. 21.

16. Daryl G. Press, "Lessons for Ground Combat in the Gulf: The Impact of Training and Technology," *International Security*, Fall 1997, p. 138.

17. Quoted in *IEEE Spectrum*, "Emulating the Battlefield," September 1991, p. 36.

★ For Further Reading ★

Books

J. Boyne, *Weapons of Desert Storm*. Lincolnwood, IL: Publications International, 1991. One of several titles intended for younger readers and focusing on the operational characteristics of weapons used in the Gulf War.

Fred Bratman, *War in the Persian Gulf*. Brookfield, CT: Millbrook, 1991. A brief but informative early account of the Gulf conflict.

Dominic J. Caraccilo, *The Ready Brigade of the 82nd Airborne in Desert Storm: A Combat Memoir by a Headquarters Company Commander*. Jefferson, NC: McFarland, 1993. A warrior's account with an emphasis on the experience of actual combat.

Frank Chadwick, *Gulf War Fact Book*. Bloomington, IL: GDW, 1991. Provides pictures, data, and brief descriptions of operational characteristics of the major weapons used in the Gulf War.

Peter Cipkowski, *Understanding the Crisis in the Persian Gulf*. New York: Wiley, 1992. A good introduction to the conflict, covering both political and military aspects.

Zachary Kent, *The Persian Gulf War: "The Mother of All Battles."* Hillside, NJ: Enslow, 1994. A general but comprehensive description and analysis of Desert Storm. Part of a series on America's wars.

John King, *The Gulf War*. Parsippany, NY: Silver Burdett, 1991. Another brief, early account of the conflict with Iraq intended for younger readers.

Website

FAS Military Analysis Network: Operation Desert Storm (www.fas.org/man/dod-101/ops/desert_storm.htm). This highly useful site of the Federation of American Scientists provides numerous links and on-line articles and documents.

✯ **Works Consulted** ✯

Books

Rick Atkinson, *Crusade: The Untold Story of the Persian Gulf War.* New York: Houghton Mifflin, 1993. A description and analysis of the war, enlivened by revelations about policy debates and dramatic depictions of combat.

James A. Baker III with Thomas M. De-Frank, *The Politics of Diplomacy: Revolution, War, and Peace, 1989-1992.* New York: Putnam's, 1995. A brief insider's account by Bush's secretary of state.

Phyllis Bennis and Michel Moushabeck, eds., *Beyond the Storm: A Gulf Crisis Reader.* New York: Olive Branch, 1991. Assorted articles on the political situation in the Persian Gulf and U.S. policy in the region by critics of U.S. foreign policy.

James Blackwell, *Thunder in the Desert: The Strategy and Tactics of the Persian Gulf War.* New York: Bantam, 1991. A CNN military analyst's early account focusing on tactics and strategy, supplemented by discussion of weapons and Iraq's military history.

Eliot A. Cohen, *Gulf War Air Power Survey.* 5 vols. Washington, DC: U.S. Government Printing Office, 1993. A massive, highly detailed independent study of airpower in the Gulf War sponsored by the U.S. Air Force.

Michael Donnelly with Denise Donnelly, *Falcon's Cry: A Desert Storm Memoir.* Westport, CT: Praeger, 1998. The Gulf War as seen by an American air force F-16 pilot.

James F. Dunnigan and Austin Bay, *From Shield to Storm: High-Tech Weapons, Military Strategy, and Coalition Warfare in the Persian Gulf.* New York: William Morrow, 1992. Two prolific authors on military affairs focus on rival weapons and forces.

Trevor N. Dupuy et al., *How to Defeat Saddam Hussein: Scenarios and Strategies for the Gulf War.* New York: Warner Books, 1991. An examination of alternative strategies for ousting Iraqis from Kuwait, written before the actual conflict by the author of numerous books on war and strategy and his colleagues.

John J. Fialka, *Hotel Warriors: Covering the Gulf.* Washington, DC: Woodrow Wilson Center, 1991. A study of press coverage of the Gulf War, concentrating on the important role of CNN and on restrictions imposed on journalists.

Lawrence Freedman and Efraim Karsh, *The Gulf Conflict, 1990-1991: Diplomacy and War in the New World Order.* Princeton, NJ: Princeton University Press, 1993. An excellent study of the political and military dimensions of the conflict.

Norman Friedman, *Desert Victory: The War for Kuwait.* Annapolis, MD: Naval Institute Press, 1991. An early but accurate military analysis with detailed accounts of weapons and battles by a respected naval expert.

John Godden, ed., *Shield and Storm: Personal Recollections of the Air War in the Gulf.* Washington and London: Brassey's, 1994. Sometimes harrowing tales of air warfare by those who participated directly in the air campaign.

Michael R. Gordon and Bernard Trainor, *The Generals' War: The Inside Story of the Conflict in the Gulf.* Boston: Little, Brown, 1995. An informed account blending military analysis and the human drama of the Gulf War.

Stephen R. Graubard, *Mr. Bush's War: Adventures in the Policies of Illusion.* New York: Hill and Wang, 1992. A critical study of Bush's policies in the Persian Gulf region.

Albert J. Mauroni, *Chemical-Biological Defense: U.S. Military Policies and Decisions in the Gulf War.* Westport, CT: Praeger, 1998. A study of U.S. efforts to cope with the possible use of chemical or biological weapons by Saddam Hussein's forces.

Douglas Menarchik, *Powerlift—Getting to Desert Storm: Strategic Transportation and Strategy in the New World Order.* Westport, CT: Praeger, 1993. A useful study of the uncelebrated but critical importance of air- and sealift in war.

John Pimlott and Stephen Badsey, *The Gulf War Assessed.* London: Sterling, 1992. An analysis of tactics and strategy by members of the Department of War Studies at the Sandhurst Royal Military Academy in Britain.

Jeffrey Record, *Hollow Victory: A Contrary View of the Gulf War.* Washington, DC: Brassey's, 1993. A critical study of Bush's strategy by a specialist on defense policy.

Robert H. Scales Jr., *Certain Victory: The U.S. Army in the Gulf War.* Washington and London: Brassey's, 1994. An army study of the war providing detailed information on tactics and battles.

H. Norman Schwarzkopf with Peter Petre, *It Doesn't Take a Hero.* New York: Bantam, 1992. A perspective on the war by the commander of CENTCOM and the coalition forces.

Micah Siffry and Christopher Cerf, eds., *The Gulf War Reader: History, Documents, Opinions.* New York: Random House, 1991. A wide-ranging collection of articles on the political aspects of the Gulf War.

Harry G. Summers Jr., *On Strategy II: A Critical Analysis of the Gulf War.* New York: Dell, 1992. A highly general study based on military historian Carl von Clausewitz's classic study of military and modeled after an earlier work by the author on Vietnam.

U.S. News & World Report, *Triumph Without Victory: The Unreported History of the Persian Gulf War.* New York: Times Books, 1992. This books explores little-known aspects of the Persian Gulf War.

Bruce W. Watson, ed., *Military Lessons of the Gulf War*. London: Greenhill Books, 1991. Another of the instant analyses of the likely effects of Desert Storm on the future of warfare.

Bob Woodward, *The Commanders*. New York: Simon and Schuster, 1991. Chapter-length studies of Colin Powell, Norman Schwarzkopf, and other Desert Storm commanders, focusing on their characters and roles in the conflict.

Periodicals

Army, "Army's Patriot: High-Tech Superstar of Desert Storm," March 1991.

Stephen Bidle, "Victory Misunderstood: What the Gulf War Tells Us About the Future of Conflict," *International Security*, Fall 1996.

Julie Bird and Tom Donnelly, "Friendly Fire," *Army Times*, September 23, 1991.

Peter Grier, "Joint Stars Does Its Stuff," *Air Force Magazine*, June 1991.

Stanley Hoffmann, "Bush Abroad," *New York Review of Books*, November 5, 1990.

IEEE Spectrum, "Emulating the Battlefield," September 1991.

————, "Warfare in the Information Age," September 1991.

Thomas A. Keaney, "The Linkage of Air and Ground Power in the Future of Conflict," *International Security*, Fall 1996.

Gary D. Langford, "Iron Rain: MLRS Storms onto the Battlefield," *Field Artillery*, December 1991.

Thomas D. Mahnken and Barry D. Watts, "What the Gulf War Can (and Cannot) Tell Us About the Future of Warfare," *International Security*, Fall 1996.

Bruce Nordwall, "U.S. Relies on Combination of Aircraft, Satellites, UAVs for Damage Assessment," *Aviation Week and Space Technology*, February 4, 1991.

Daryl G. Press, "Lessons for Ground Combat in the Gulf: The Impact of Training and Technology," *International Security*, Fall 1997.

Jimmy D. Ross, "Victory: The Logistics Story," *Army*, October 1991.

Robert H. Scales Jr., "Accuracy Defeated Range in Artillery Duel," *International Defense Review*, May 1991.

Ben F. Schemmer, "USAF MH-53J Pave Lows Led Army Apaches Knocking Out Iraqi Radars to Open Air War," *Armed Forces Journal International*, July 1991.

Michael Sterner, "Closing the Gate: The Persian Gulf War Revisited," *Current History*, January 1997.

Douglas Waller, "Secret Warriors," *Newsweek*, June 17, 1991.

Website

Military Equipment of the Former USSR "Surface to Air Missile (SAMs) Systems." (www.armscontrol.ru/atmtc/Arms_systems/Land/Missiles/SAM/airdef.htm#sa-2).

★ Index ★

★ Picture Credits ★

Cover photo: © Corbis
© Aero Graphics, Inc./Corbis, 38, 42, 47 (right)
© AFP/Corbis, 9, 11 (left), 23, 27, 67
AP/Wide World Photos, 11 (right), 33, 35, 36
Archive Photos/Imapress, 39
© Bettmann/Corbis, 10
© Corbis, 7, 13, 17 (right), 18, 25, 31, 40, 43, 50, 51, 52, 58, 68, 73
FPG International, 66, 88
© George Hall/Corbis, 47 (left)
Imapress/Gauthier/Archive Photos, 26, 90, 91
© Martin McKenzie; The Military Picture Library/Corbis, 44
Francoise de Muler/Corbis, 14
© Museum of Flight/Corbis, 17 (left)
© Reuters NewMedia/Corbis, 55
Reuters/Pat Benic/Archive Photos, 65
Reuters/Greg Bos/Archive Photos, 84
Reuters/D.O.D./Greg Bos/Archive Photos, 97
Reuters/Richard Ellis/Archive Photos, 28
Reuters/Jim Hollander/Archive Photos, 82, 86
Reuters/Reinhard Krause/Archive Photos, 32, 93, 94
Reuters/Win McNammee/Archive Photos, 56, 95
Reuters/Claude Salani/Archive Photos, 77
Reuters/Phillipe Wojazer/Archive Photos, 60
© Leif Skoogfors/Corbis, 75, 76
© Peter Turnley/Corbis, 64, 71, 80

☆ About the Author ☆

Jay Speakman earned a Ph.D. in political science from Columbia University. He specializes in international relations and has taught at Rutgers University, Claremont McKenna College, Pomona College, Northeastern University, and the University of Massachusetts, Boston. His research and teaching focus on European affairs, American foreign and national security politics, and international environmental politics. Dr. Speakman and his wife, June, live in Barrington, Rhode Island with their two sons, Jason and Adam. Dr. Speakman spends much of his free time coaching his sons' baseball and basketball teams.